THE VALUE OF MONEY

ELLEN R. FEINGOLD

A SMITHSONIAN CONTRIBUTION TO KNOWLEDGE

Smithsonian Institution
Scholarly Press

WASHINGTON, D.C.
2015

Published by
SMITHSONIAN INSTITUTION SCHOLARLY PRESS
P.O. Box 37012, MRC 957
Washington, D.C. 20013-7012
www.scholarlypress.si.edu

All photos by Jaclyn Nash unless otherwise credited.
All images courtesy of the National Museum of American History unless otherwise credited.

The objects that appear in this book have been enlarged and reduced in size. Information about the actual dimensions of objects in the National Numismatic Collection is available on the National Museum of American History's website www. americanhistory.si.edu.

Cover and title page image: Eight real coin, Mexico, 1762 (Figure 73b on p. 50). Eight real coins were widespread in colonial America and were the world's first global currency. They reflect and symbolize both American history and global history.

Library of Congress Cataloging-in-Publication Data
Feingold, Ellen R. (Ellen Roseanne), 1983–
The value of money / Ellen R. Feingold.
pages cm
"A Smithsonian contribution to knowledge."
Includes bibliographical references and index.
ISBN 978-1-935623-80-9 (cloth : alkaline paper) — ISBN 978-1-935623-81-6 (ebook)
1. Numismatics—Exhibitions. 2. Money—Exhibitions. 3. Coins—Exhibitions. 4. Paper money—Exhibitions. 5. Coins—History—Exhibitions. 6. Money—History—Exhibitions. 7. Coins—Collectors and collecting—Exhibitions. 8. Money—Collectors and collecting—Exhibitions. 9. National Numismatic Collection (U.S.)—Catalogs. I. Title.
CJ41.W38F45 2015
737—dc23

2015010822

ISBN-13 (cloth): 978-1-935623-80-9
ISBN-13 (ebook): 978-1-935623-81-6

Printed in Canada

♾ The paper used in this publication meets the minimum requirements of the American National Standard for Permanence of Paper for Printed Library Materials Z39.48–1992.

CONTENTS

INTRODUCTION

The story of money is a global one. For thousands of years, communities around the world have designated objects to represent value and facilitate transactions. Objects that at first seem to have no relationship to one another—tiny metal coins, massive stones, and colorful seashells—have become associated through their use as money, connecting them and the communities that used them through this shared aspect of human history.

The practice of collecting monetary objects, both by individuals and by museums, has brought together a vast range of material and created "money collections," with which local and national histories can be compared in the context of wider global histories. The National Numismatic Collection, the Smithsonian Institution's collection of money, is one of those collections. Composed of approximately one and a half million objects, its holdings represent every inhabited continent and span more than 2,600 years.

The National Numismatic Collection's vault contains the objects many would expect to find in a money collection—namely, metal coins and paper notes. But it also holds other forms of money and objects that are related to the history of money and exchange. Coin dies and molds, sketches, plasters, and printing plates are part of the collection and capture the history of the production processes for creating coins and notes. The collection also includes official financial documents and apparatuses, such as bonds, personal checks and banking materials, and historic correspondence relating to the American financial system, as well as financial ephemera and temporary currencies. These objects are housed with a remarkable range of commodity or "traditional" currencies such as wampum, bricks of tea, bars of salt, animal pelts, and feathers. Twentieth- and twenty-first-century innovations, such as credit cards and readers, are also among the holdings, reflecting the new and rapidly changing technologies of money. Jewelry made from money (Figure 1), art and commemorative medals, orders, and decorations are part of this collection too. Although medals are not money, they have historically been included in the field of numismatics because of their similarity to coins in their size, metal composition, and design.[1] Medals also offer opportunities to make connections between monetary objects and sculptural art and design as well as political and social history.

Figure 1.
Gold coin necklace, United States, twentieth century. Donated by Estate of Doris M. Brixey.

The bulk of this diverse collection was acquired by the Smithsonian after 1950, but numismatic objects have been part of the institution since its establishment in 1846. Over the last century and a half, the collection has grown from a few thousand objects in its early years to about a million and a half today. The development of this collection can be traced alongside the growth of the Smithsonian Institution's other collections and buildings. Monetary objects and medals were initially housed with and considered part of the Smithsonian's broader history collections in the National Mall's famous red brick building, the Smithsonian Institution Building, also known as "the Castle."[2] In the early 1880s, these objects were moved to the National Museum Building (now called the Arts and Industries Building), which was constructed to house the Smithsonian's acquisition of materials from the 1876 Centennial Exposition held in Philadelphia.[3] The numismatic collection remained there for nearly a century until the completion of the Museum of History and Technology in 1964. Perfectly placed in this new museum with a focus on both history and technology—the pillars of numismatics—the international collection found its permanent home. In 1980, however, the museum was renamed the National Museum of American History and became the foremost institution in the nation dedicated to exploring and understanding the American experience. Since then, some have wondered how useful an international collection of money can be to a museum about American history.

The Value of Money exhibition celebrates the value of having a geographically and chronologically diverse numismatic collection in the National Museum of American History. It demonstrates the power of using monetary objects to explore American history and its connections to global histories of exchange, cultural interaction and expression, political change, and innovation. By integrating American objects with objects from around the world spanning nearly three millennia, the exhibition uses money as a vehicle to engage with not only the American experience but also the human experience. It embraces the world cultures and practices that have made monetary objects at once so diverse and so similar.

This new exhibition continues a long tradition of galleries and displays featuring the Smithsonian's numismatic treasures. The small numismatic collection of the nineteenth century was first shown in the Castle and later, intermittently, in the National Museum Building in traditional numismatic style with displays organized by country or region, metal, and denomination.[4] Donations of foreign coins from officials, such as President Ulysses S. Grant's collection of Japanese coins, and from private individuals, such as George B. Glover's collection of East Asian coins, allowed curators to feature beautiful and rare international material from an early stage.

In 1914, the Smithsonian installed its first major numismatic gallery, showing more than 6,000 coins, medals, and tokens—a significant portion of the collection at the time.[5] The numismatic display was then substantially enhanced

Figure 2.
One sovereign coin, England, 1558–1603. Transfer from U.S. Mint.

through the addition of many objects that arrived with the historic transfer of the Philadelphia Mint's collection in 1923. Totaling more than 18,300 pieces, the Mint's collection included patterns, proofs, private gold issues from the Gold Rush era, and rare ancient and modern coins from America, Europe (Figure 2), Latin America, and elsewhere, as well as medals and decorations.[6] This transfer nearly doubled the size of the Smithsonian's numismatic holdings and gave it some of America's rarest coins.

The addition of the Mint's collection was a watershed for numismatics at the Smithsonian. It helped to raise the numismatic collection's profile, and in 1948, numismatics became a separate division with a dedicated curator, Stuart Mosher.[7] Committed to building the national collection, Mosher cultivated relationships with private collectors, not only acquiring their collections but also working with them to fill gaps in the national collection. During Mosher's tenure, Paul A. Straub (Figure 3), an avid collector of gold and silver coins from fourteenth- to twentieth-century Europe, donated his personal collection of approximately 5,650 coins to the Smithsonian.[8] Even after this generous gift, he continued to work with Mosher to acquire coins that would enhance the Smithsonian's European holdings. His donations helped bring the Smithsonian's collection "competitively

Figure 3.
Collector and donor Paul A. Straub.

into the field of international numismatics" by adding the kinds of materials held in the famous coin cabinets of London, Paris, and Berlin.[9]

Mosher's commitment to his work greatly enhanced the numismatic collection, but the dedication of his successors, Vladimir Clain-Stefanelli and Elvira Clain-Stefanelli, to developing the size, diversity, and strength of the collection made it one of the largest and most diverse numismatic collections in the world. The arrival of this husband and wife team at the Smithsonian in the mid-1950s marked a turning point in the development and display of the collection.

The Clain-Stefanellis regarded money as a central and enduring feature of human history, one which could be traced from an evolutionary perspective. This point of view shaped the way in which they curated the Hall of Monetary History and Medallic Art, installed in the Museum of History and Technology in 1964 (Figure 4). This hall, which was redesigned in the early 1970s, became the core of the Smithsonian's numismatic display for more than 40 years.[10] It emphasized "the numismatic contribution to history, economic theory and practice, and the development of art" over time.[11] The Clain-Stefanellis structured the exhibit around chronology as well as specific historical periods and topics like the Reformation and the Confederacy.

The display was refreshed and enhanced over time by the enormous quantity of new material donated by individual collectors and institutions during the second half of the twentieth century. The sheer numbers are impressive—growing the collection from around 64,000 objects to around 900,000 objects

Figure 4.
The Hall of Monetary History and Medallic Art at the Museum of History and Technology.

during the Clain-Stefanellis' tenure—but the quality and rarity of some of the material is awe-inspiring.[12] A full list of significant acquisitions is too lengthy to include here, but it will suffice to note that a great deal of the material for which the National Numismatic Collection is now known was collected by the Clain-Stefanellis (Figure 5).[13] Some of the highlights include Catherine Bullowa's donation of 21,000 objects, including many world coins; Mortimer Neinken's donation of a wide variety of ancient coins and more than 100,000 international notes; Willis du Pont's donation of the Georgii Mikhailovich Collection of approximately 11,400 Russian coins and medals, thought to be the strongest outside of Russia; R. Henry Norweb and Emery May Norweb's collection of rare American and English coins and tokens (Figure 6); the Stack family's donations of approximately 62,000 American and international coins, tokens, medals, notes, and alternative currencies; and Alfred Bloomingdale's donation of early credit cards and original cartoons about consumer credit. Among this impressive list, the 1968 acquisition of the Josiah K. Lilly Jr. Collection of 6,125 gold coins stands out not only because it significantly enhanced the American and international gold coin holdings (Figure 7) but also because it became a key feature of the Smithsonian's numismatic display. The Clain-Stefanellis' display of Lilly's gold (Figure 8) is remembered by many American numismatists today as the source of inspiration for their personal collections.[14]

In addition to the collections acquired from individuals, the Clain-Stefanellis acquired three major institutional collections. The Bureau of

Figure 5.
Vladimir Clain-Stefanelli (left) and Elvira Clain-Stefanelli (right) receiving a donation of Austrian notgeld from Sol Kaplan (middle) in 1966.

Figure 6.
Five cent "Liberty Head Nickel" coin, United States, 1913. Donated by R. Henry Norweb.

Figure 7.
Twenty dollar "Ultra High Relief Double Eagle" coin, United States, 1907. Donated by Estate of Josiah K. Lilly Jr.

Figure 8.
The Josiah K. Lilly Jr. Collection of gold coins on display.

Engraving and Printing transferred its collection of record consisting of approximately 300,000 certified proofs of national bank notes and many other forms of paper money and tax stamps to the division between 1966 and 1980. In 1978, the U.S. Treasury also transferred its collection of paper money (Figures 9 and 10), which comprised 808 federal notes, many in pristine condition. That same year, The Chase Manhattan Bank donated its significant collection of approximately 24,000 objects, including coins, notes, banking materials, and a tremendous range of commodity money from cultures around the world (Figures 11 and 12).[15] The collection was so vast and impressive that it had its own museum, called The Chase Manhattan Bank Money Museum, at Rockefeller Center in New York City, before it was donated to the Smithsonian. This gift gave the National Numismatic Collection some of the objects that are most popular with nonnumismatists, such as the famous stone money of the island of Yap and an extensive collection of personal checks from many of America's presidents. The Clain-Stefanellis also initiated the acquisition of approximately 600,000 notes and related financial instruments issued by the Confederate States of America. This group of objects, often referred to as the "Richmond Hoard" because it was seized by Union authorities in Richmond, Virginia, at the end of the Civil War, was first transferred from the U.S. Treasury to the National Archives and then later to the Smithsonian in 1998.[16]

Figure 9.
One hundred thousand dollar gold certificate, United States, 1934. Donated by U.S. Department of the Treasury.

Figure 10.
One thousand dollar "Grand Watermelon" Treasury note, United States, 1890. Donated by U.S. Department of the Treasury.

Figure 11.
Copper cross, central and southern Africa, nineteenth century. Donated by The Chase Manhattan Bank.

Figure 12.
Coin tree mold, China, 1862–1874. Donated by The Chase Manhattan Bank.

In 1982, Vladimir Clain-Stefanelli passed away, and Elvira Clain-Stefanelli became the lead curator, continuing to collect and develop topical numismatic displays with her colleagues in the National Museum of American History until her retirement in 2000. Shortly after her retirement, in 2004 the National Museum of American History began a long-term renovation and revitalization of its displays, which involved taking down numerous exhibitions, including the Clain-Stefanellis' hall. In the years that followed, Clain-Stefanelli's successor and longstanding colleague, Richard Doty, installed two small numismatic displays, *Legendary Coins and Currency* in 2005 then *Stories on Money* in 2009, both focusing largely on American money. The latter particularly sought to highlight the relationship between American money and people, emphasizing Doty's interest in the study of human relationships to monetary objects. These exhibitions helped galvanize the numismatic community to support the development of a larger gallery with up-to-date display techniques and the opportunity to show more of the vast collection.

The Value of Money reflects many generations of commitment to growing the National Numismatic Collection and a broad base of support for its display. It builds on previous approaches to numismatic display at the Smithsonian while also offering a new perspective on how the collection can be used to explore history. This approach to interpreting the collection emphasizes that monetary objects are objects of interaction. Through these objects, the relationships among individuals, communities, and governments and their citizens can be explored, and the geographic boundaries that have constrained display in the past can be crossed. Thus, money from the United States of America is paired with money from around the world to explore the relationships between peoples, places, and ideas.

The Value of Money exhibition is organized into five thematic sections reflected in this work by chapters. It begins with the origins of money, which explores the variety of forms of money and materials used to make monetary objects throughout history, highlighting that coins and notes have circulated alongside other forms of money for centuries. It suggests that the use of an object and the relationship people have to it, rather than its material form, are the essence of its function as money. The second chapter traces how twentieth- and twenty-first-century innovations in money, both digital and physical, are altering how people conduct commerce and the form of money they rely on. New technologies of money, from credit cards to cryptocurrencies, are diminishing some types of human interaction around transactions while also creating new connections and relationships across large geographic distances. Innovations in coins and notes, such as the creation of the euro and plastic notes, are shifting long-standing notions about who can issue currency and what materials make monetary objects secure enough to trust. The third chapter focuses on the political, social, and cultural messages money conveys through words and images placed on money and through currencies issued for specific circumstances. The ubiquity of money makes it both an effective means of communication for political leaders and a powerful means through which both cultural and political ideas and ideals of community, identity, and heritage can be conveyed and defined. The fourth chapter looks at the artistry of coins and notes. It explores how the addition of purposeful and symbolic art is used to convey the importance of money in society and to honor people, commemorate significant events, and inspire respect and loyalty to governments. The final chapter focuses on the allure of money to collectors. Among the many objects that are popular to collect, monetary objects, particularly coins, have a unique appeal. They invoke a feeling of connection to people and places from the past and symbolize moments in personal or general history. Few historic objects are at once so powerful and accessible. It is this rare quality that has inspired so many to build their own collections and, for some, to donate them to the National Numismatic Collection. This collection of collections has become a reservoir for building a new understanding of the history and passion of the practice of money collecting.

The objects in *The Value of Money* include some that have been at the heart of numismatic display at the Smithsonian since its early years and some that have emerged from the vault for the first time. By blending the familiar with the unfamiliar, the brand-new with the old, and the American with the international, *The Value of Money* aims to inspire people to look for the history behind money and see it in a global context.

THE ORIGINS OF MONEY

All money is a matter of belief.
—George J. W. Goodman, American editorialist[1]

Money is defined by economists as a medium of exchange, a store of value, and a unit of account. Simply put, money is something that can be used to make a payment.[2] Any object can serve this purpose as long as it has an agreed-upon value and is trusted for use in transactions. Many different objects have functioned as money throughout history, reflecting the various ways that communities have designated value as well as illustrating how ideas about worth have changed over time.

Seashells, bricks of tea, bars of salt, stones, and plastic cards are just some of the many nonmetallic objects that have been used to make payments. Small objects, such as cowrie shells, once circulated across significant trade networks in Africa and Asia, whereas large, heavy objects, such as doughnut-shaped stones from the island of Yap, were exchanged only among the local community. Precious metals and base metals have also been used to make money. Although coins are the most common today, metallic money has taken many forms, such as copper crosses from southern Africa and silver bars from Laos. Monetary objects in forms other than coins and notes are often referred to as "primitive" or "traditional" money, yet they are essentially the same as coins and notes in their function and utility to the societies that have relied on them. They have also circulated alongside coins and notes for millennia.

The use of metal coins can be traced back more than 2,600 years to tiny stamped pieces of electrum—a naturally occurring mixture of gold and silver—in ancient Lydia (modern Turkey) and small bronze tools in China. Until the mid-twentieth century, many governments around the world issued coins made from gold and silver. The scarcity and desirability of precious metals made gold and silver coins intrinsically valuable but also constrained monetary supplies, forcing governments and their citizens to rely on alternative forms of money.[3]

Paper money was first used in China more than 1,000 years ago. Beginning in the seventeenth century, governments and banks in Europe and America increasingly printed and issued paper money. Some governments cultivated trust in paper by making it redeemable for precious metal coins and bullion. For example, the United States issued gold certificates from 1865 to 1934 and silver certificates from 1878 to 1964. Over the last century, governments around the world abandoned the practice of connecting gold and silver to the value of their currencies in favor of fiat currencies. Fiat currencies do not derive value from the materials used, but rather from their legal status as currency and public trust in the issuing government.

Whether a carefully engraved note or string of colorful beads made from shells, in order for objects to work as money, people have to believe in them. When a society collectively agrees on the value of money, trade can take place and wealth can accumulate. The great diversity in size, form, material, and design of money used around the world demonstrates that its origins do not lie in a particular object or place but in shared understandings between individuals and communities.

FORMS OF MONEY

Nonmetallic Money

Feathers, bones, seashells, cloth, and important commodities, such as bricks of tea (Figure 13), are just some of the various objects that have been used to represent value and to make general or ceremonial payments. Some objects, such as seashells (Figure 14), have been used as money both in their original form and as raw material to make monetary objects, such as Native American wampum (Figure 15).

Figure 13.
Brick of tea, Siberia, eighteenth to nineteenth century. Donated by the Stack family.

Figure 14.
Cowrie shells. Donated by The Chase Manhattan Bank.

Figure 15.
Clam shell wampum, United States. Donated by The Chase Manhattan Bank.

Seashell Money

Small seashells have many characteristics that make them ideal monetary objects. They are durable, portable, and difficult to imitate. One species of cowrie shell is named *Cypraea moneta,* or the money cowrie, because it was used so widely for this purpose (Figure 16). Shells circulated as a medium of exchange in Asia, Africa, Oceania, and North America. Seashells are no longer an official form of money, but they remain an alternative to notes and coins during periods of scarcity. During the Great Depression, decorated clam shells briefly functioned as money in Pismo Beach, California (Figure 17).

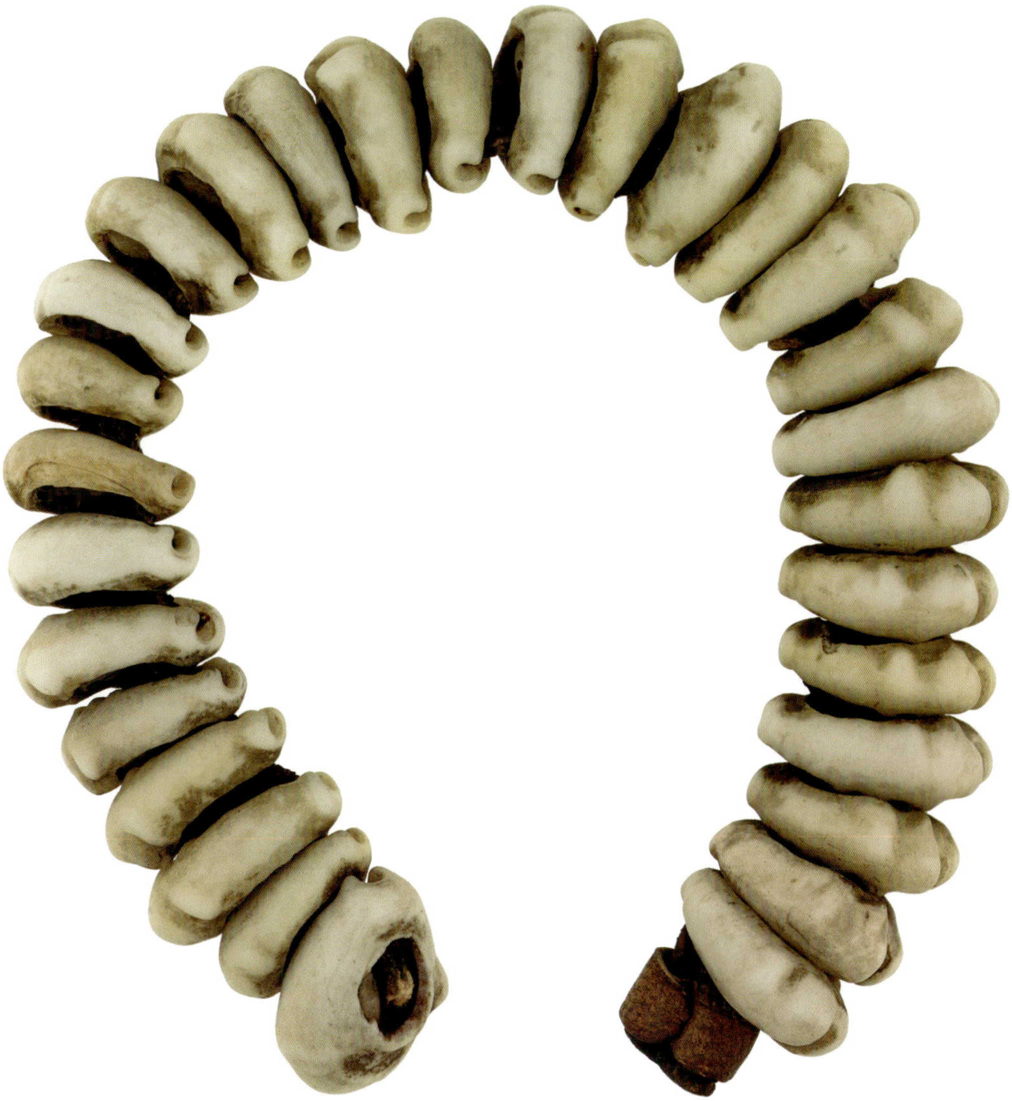

Figure 16.
Twenty-nine strung cowrie shells. Donated by The Chase Manhattan Bank.

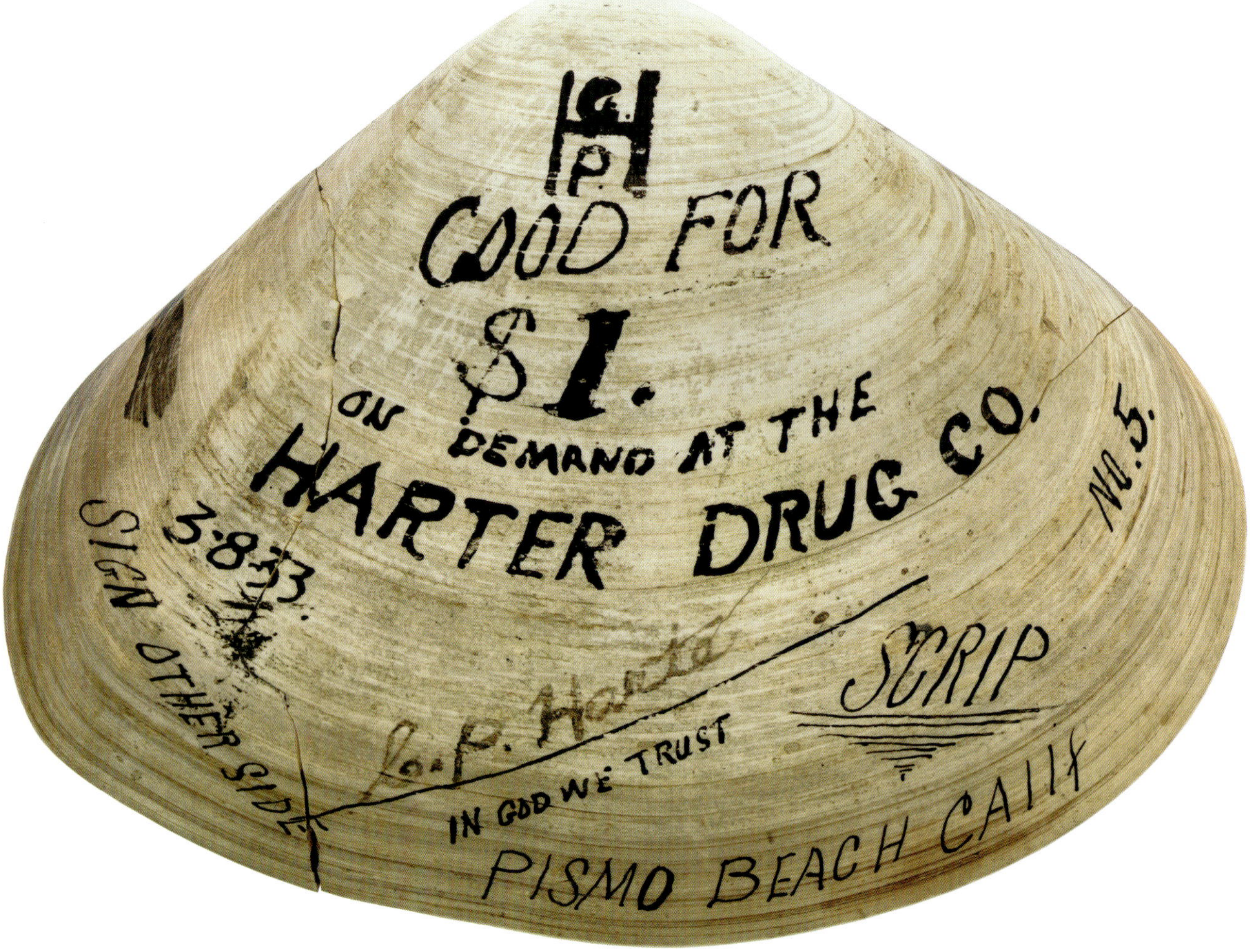

Figure 17.
One dollar clam shell, United States, 1933. Donated by The Chase Manhattan Bank.

Stone Money from the Island of Yap

Stone rings, called rai, have been used as money on the Pacific island of Yap. The rai shown in Figure 18 weighs 168.5 pounds and measures about 28 inches across. It is not intended to circulate like a coin. Instead, its use has been reserved for significant or ceremonial payments, such as dowries and funerary payments (Figure 19). Rai have also represented accumulated wealth and conveyed social status. Some stone rings are so large and heavy that they cannot be moved, but changes in ownership of the rings are acknowledged by the community on Yap.[4]

Figure 18.
Stone ring, island of Yap (Micronesia), twentieth century. Donated by The Chase Manhattan Bank.

Figure 19.
Stone money with strings of pearl shell "presented to a corpse at a burial." Photo reproduced from W. H. Furness, "The Stone Money of Uap, West Caroline Islands," Transactions of the Department of Archaeology, University of Pennsylvania Museum *1 (1904): 57.*

Metallic Money

Many different metals have been used as money, including copper, iron, tin, gold, and silver. Metal money is durable and can be melted down and used for other purposes, which makes it an appealing form of payment. Metallic money ranges from simple shapes to highly refined designs (Figures 20–22).

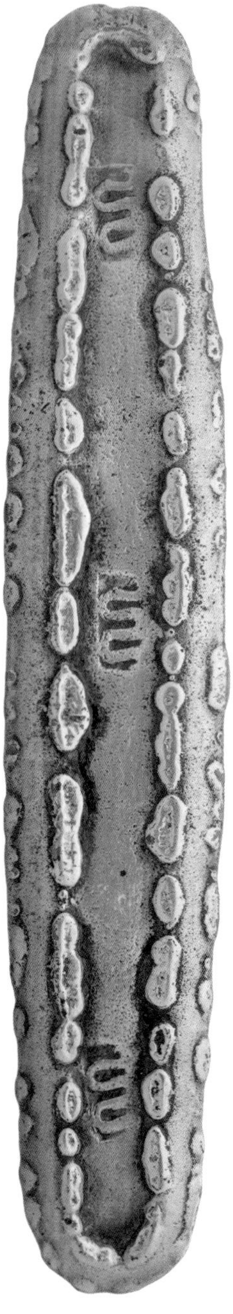

Figure 20.
Silver "Tiger's Tongue" bar ingot, Laos, nineteenth century. Donated by The Chase Manhattan Bank.

Figure 21.
Manilla, West Africa, nineteenth century. Donated by The Chase Manhattan Bank.

Figure 22.
"Tin Hat" coin, Malay Peninsula, nineteenth century. Donated by Mrs. F. C .C. Boyd.

Iron Money

Kissi pennies are made from iron and take their name from the Kissi people of modern-day Liberia and Sierra Leone (Figure 23). It is believed that the shape was intended to display the quality of the iron. The shape shows that the iron can be twisted, hammered, sharpened into a blade, and fashioned into points.[5] Kissi pennies were used for transactions in West Africa from the nineteenth to the mid-twentieth century and could be exchanged for coins and notes circulating in the region.

Figure 23.
Kissi pennies, Liberia, nineteenth to twentieth century. Donated by The Chase Manhattan Bank.

The Origins of Coins

The earliest coins originated independently in three different parts of the world. Around the same time in the seventh century BCE, coins were first made in Lydia (modern Turkey) and in China. The first Indian coins were made in the fifth century BCE. The earliest coins from Lydia (Figure 24) and India (Figure 25) were made from small, round pieces of metal, whereas the first Chinese coins were in the shape of farming tools, such as the bronze spade in Figure 26.

Figure 24.
One-third stater coin, Lydia, seventh to sixth century BCE.
Donated by Estate of Josiah K. Lilly Jr.

Figure 25.
Punch-marked coin, Son River region (India), fourth century BCE.
Donated by Raymond and Meryem Hebert.

Figure 26.
Hollow-handle spade, China, fifth to fourth century BCE*. Donated by George B. Glover.*

The Origins of Paper Money

Paper money as it is known today was first developed in China in the eleventh century. The note in Figure 27 was issued by the Ming dynasty in the fourteenth century. Its value corresponded to 1,000 bronze coins, which are depicted strung together in the center of the note.[6]

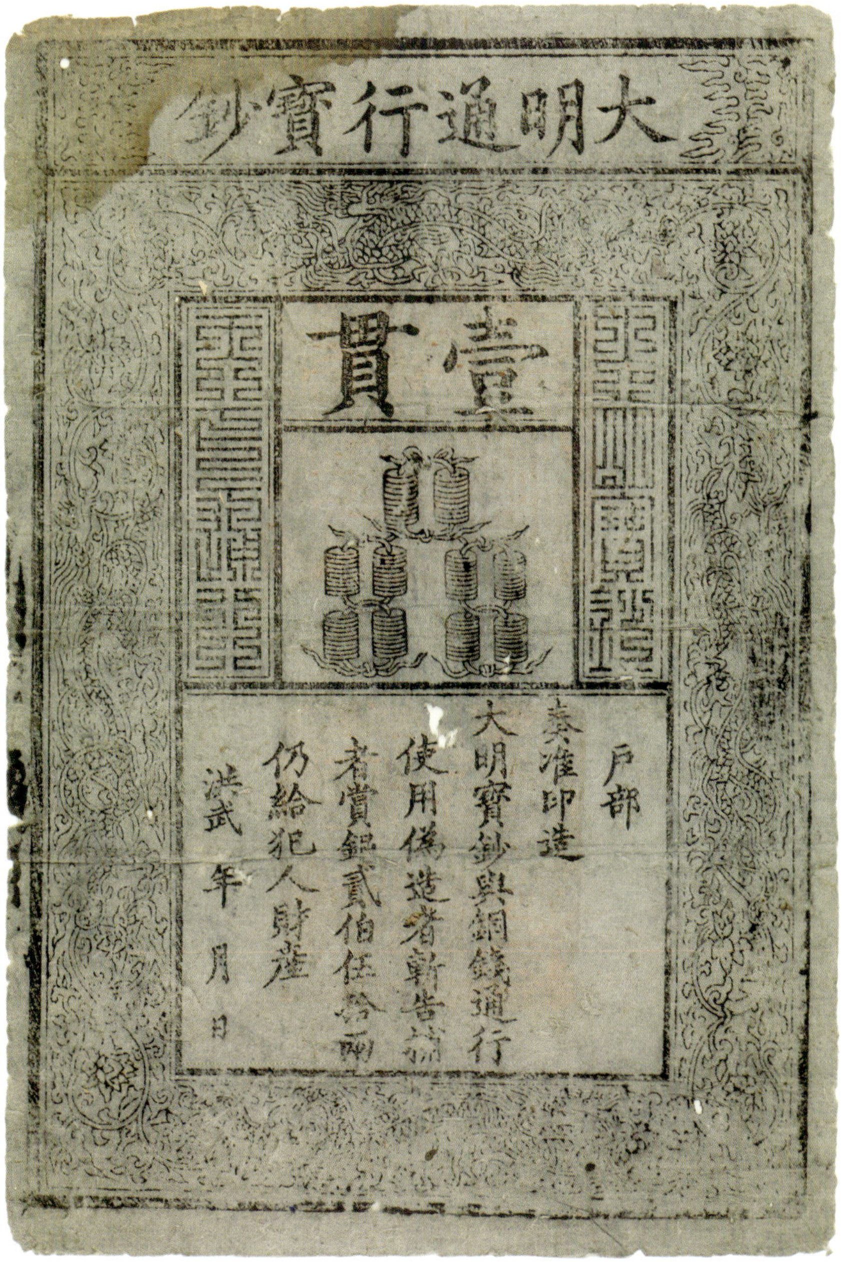

Figure 27.
Great Ming Circulating Treasure Note, China, fourteenth century. Donated by The Chase Manhattan Bank.

PRECIOUS METALS AND MONEY

Weighing Metals

The weight and purity of precious metal, such as gold and silver, determines its value as money. Determining weight requires a scale (Figure 28) and a trustworthy set of weights of known measurements. Some cultures have made weights into art forms, such as sculptural weights that were used in West Africa for weighing gold dust from the fifteenth century to the late nineteenth century (Figures 29 and 30).[7]

Figure 28.
Scale, United States, nineteenth century.

Figure 29.
Crocodile gold weight, Gold Coast (Ghana), nineteenth century. Donated by Benjamin and Harvey G. Stack.

Figure 30.
Shield gold weight, Gold Coast (Ghana), nineteenth century. Donated by National Museum of African Art, Smithsonian Institution.

Gold and Silver

The use of gold and silver in transactions can be traced back more than 4,000 years to ancient Mesopotamia and Egypt. These precious metals are valued for their scarcity, making them desirable materials for saving and trading. Gold and silver became the most widely used precious metals for coins in the ancient world and were regularly used to make coins until the mid-twentieth century (Figures 31–35).

Figure 31.
Gold ingot, Mexico, seventeenth century. Donated by Franklin P. Perdue.

Figure 32.
Eight escudo coin, Mexico, 1744. Donated by Estate of Josiah K. Lilly Jr.

Figure 33.
Silver ingot, China, late nineteenth century. Donated by The Chase Manhattan Bank.

Figure 34.
Tetradrachm coin, Athens, 454–404 BCE.

Figure 35.
Stater coin, Corinth, fourth century BCE. Transfer from U.S. Mint.

Precious Metals and Paper Money

The scarcity of gold and silver, precious metals used in the production of coins, constrained monetary supplies. From the seventeenth century, governments increasingly began to issue paper money, which could be redeemed for gold or silver coins or bullion. The notes in Figures 36 and 37 are gold and silver certificates issued in the United States during the late nineteenth and early twentieth centuries.

Figure 36.
Twenty dollar gold certificate, United States, 1905. Donated by The Chase Manhattan Bank.

Figure 37.
Five dollar silver certificate, United States, 1886. Donated by U.S. Department of the Treasury.

Fiat Currency

Precious metals are no longer used to make national currencies or to back them. Today, money derives its value from national laws defining what can be used as legal tender and the user's faith in the authority that issues that money. This type of money is referred to as fiat, which means "it shall be" in Latin (Figure 38).

Figure 38.
One dollar note, United States, 1963. Donated by Mr. and Mrs. Charles O'Donnell.

MINTING AND PRINTING MONEY

Minting Coins

Coins can be made by casting metal in a mold or striking metal between two dies. Coin dies are made from hard metals, including bronze, iron, and steel, and are engraved with negative impressions (Figure 39).[8] Each pair of dies has different designs for the obverse, or front, and reverse of a coin. Coins were struck by hand with a hammer until the sixteenth century, when the process became increasingly mechanized.

Figure 39.
One cent coin dies, Confederate States of America, 1861. Donated by Robert Bashlow.

Printing Notes

Notes are made using printing plates, which are coated with ink and pressed into special paper, leaving behind a design that is intended to be easy to recognize but difficult to forge.[9] Early printing plates were made from copper, such as the twenty dollar Confederate printing plate from 1861 shown in Figure 40. It was used to print Confederate currency during the American Civil War.

Figure 40.
Twenty dollar note printing plate, Confederate States of America, 1861.

THE INNOVATIONS OF MONEY

For the importance of money essentially flows from its being a link between the present and the future.
—John Maynard Keynes, British economist[1]

Cash has long been considered the most dependable way to receive payment. However, over the last century the number of cashless transactions has been rapidly increasing because of the innovations of credit cards and digital payment systems. Around the world, emerging monetary technologies are increasingly allowing individuals to make payments via their phones, tablets, and computers. By changing how people make payments, these new technologies are also affecting how people interact with each other and conduct commerce, both locally and globally.

Over the course of the twentieth century, new technologies gave American consumers more options in making payments, the most significant of which were charge and credit cards. Consumers were first able to make payments at particular stores and restaurants with Charga-Plate and Diners' Club and later in a much broader range of businesses through general-purpose charge and credit cards. Early plates and cards, first made from metal, paper, and cardboard, were increasingly replaced with plastic cards starting in the early 1960s. Since its invention, the plastic credit card has itself evolved, with the addition of the magnetic stripe in the 1970s and 1980s and the more recent Chip and PIN security technology widespread in Europe today. Alongside changes in plastic cards, credit card readers have also transformed. The emergence of payment dongles, such as the Square Reader and Paypal Here, allows individuals and businesses to accept credit and debit card payments via applications on smartphones and tablets, reducing the investment cost relative to traditional credit card machines.

The growth in credit card technology has altered how people with access to credit and banking infrastructure carry out transactions, but these methods of payment are inaccessible to many people around the world. The spread of mobile phones, however, has provided a platform for new payment systems that do not require access to a bank account or credit. Mobile money systems, first introduced in Kenya in 2007, are now available in many countries across Africa, South and Central America, and Asia. In countries where mobile money has become prevalent, it provides an accessible alternative to cash and a relatively secure method of storing earnings and making payments. New products for saving and borrowing via mobile money systems are also presenting new opportunities for greater financial inclusion for the world's poor.[2]

Among these cutting-edge technologies of money, few have captivated and confused people more than cryptocurrencies, such as Bitcoin. Although not widely accepted, cryptocurrencies have recently garnered a significant amount of media attention because they are not regulated by any government or single authority, and they offer an anonymous means of making payments online.

Despite the great variety of established and emerging digital technologies, cash remains a trusted and, in some cases, more readily accepted form of payment around the world. To maintain trust in cash, governments continue to develop new techniques for the design and production of coins and notes intended to make them harder to counterfeit. The addition of new security features to paper notes and the use of plastic notes with security features unachievable with paper, such as embedded clear lenses, are affecting how notes both look and feel.

Political changes are also affecting monetary objects, causing the creation of new currencies while eliminating others. Some of the world's newest nations, such as the Republic of South Sudan, have chosen to issue their own currencies to celebrate and solidify their independence. At the same time, however, the establishment and spread of the euro—the regional currency now used by much of Europe—is continuously reducing the number of European currencies and the total number of national currencies in the world.

All of these transformations have resulted in a remarkable range of objects. Together, they tell the story of the powerful impact that the innovations of money had on the twentieth century and the ways in which they are already shaping the twenty-first century.

Store Cards

Store cards were introduced in the United States in the early twentieth century. The invention of the metal Charga-Plate in 1928 mechanized the process of a customer making payments on an account at a particular store (Figures 41–42). Diners' Club, established in 1950, offered customers a single card to pay at multiple high-end businesses, first in the United States and later internationally (Figure 43).

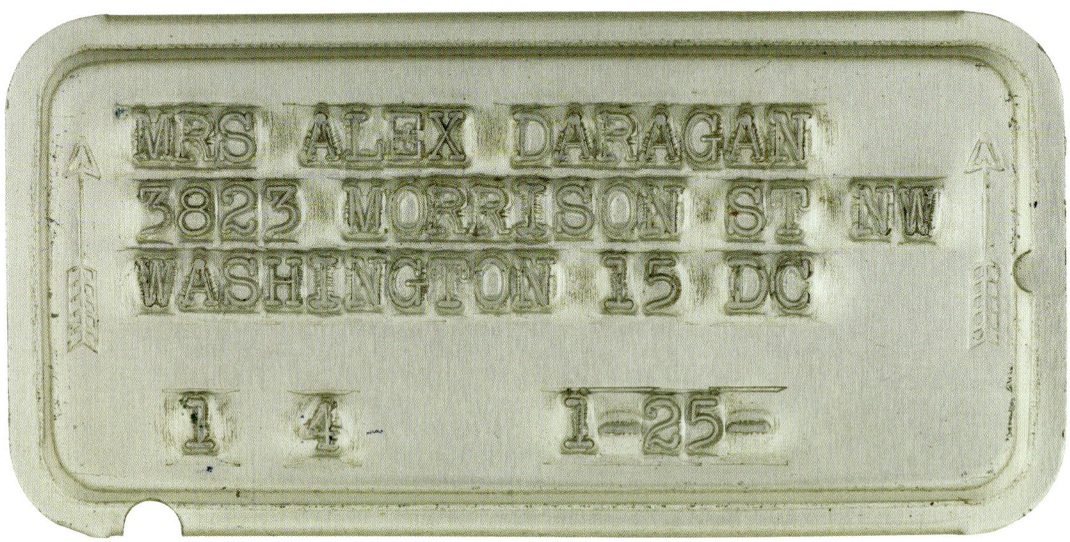

Figure 41.
Charga-Plate, United States, 1960s. Donated by Joseph and Nancy W. Daragan.

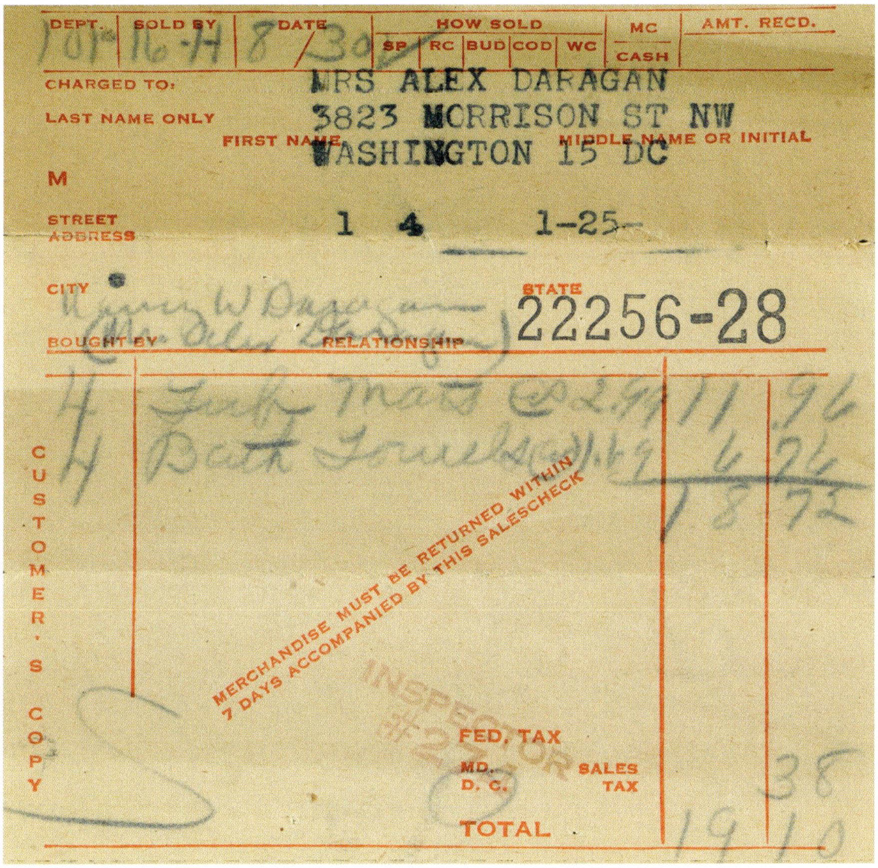

Figure 42.
Charga-Plate receipt, United States, 1960s. Donated by Joseph and Nancy W. Daragan.

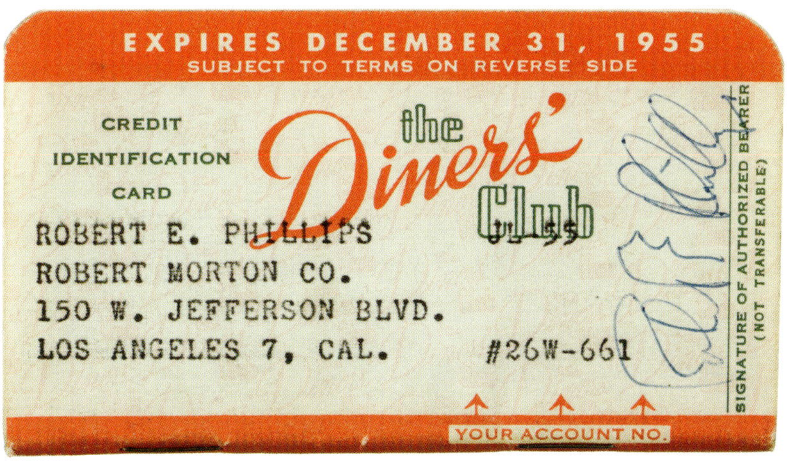

Figure 43.
Diners' Club card, United States, 1955. Donated by Alfred Bloomingdale.

General-Purpose Charge and Credit Cards

General-purpose charge and credit cards were first developed in the United States. The BankAmericard (now Visa) and American Express card became available to consumers in the late 1950s (Figure 44). Master Charge (now MasterCard) followed in 1966 (Figure 45). Some early charge and credit cards were made from paper or cardboard, but since the 1960s they have typically been made from plastic.

Figure 44.
Sample American Express card, United States, 1958. Image courtesy of American Express Corporate Archives.

Figure 45.
Master Charge card, United States, circa 1978. Donated by Elvira Clain-Stefanelli.

Magnetic Stripe Credit Cards

The addition of a magnetic stripe to plastic credit cards in the 1970s and 1980s made the payment process faster and more secure for customers and merchants (Figure 46). Electronic credit card readers work by automatically decoding personal and financial information embedded in the magnetic stripe (Figure 47). The stripe technology helped to spread the use of credit cards to countries around the world.

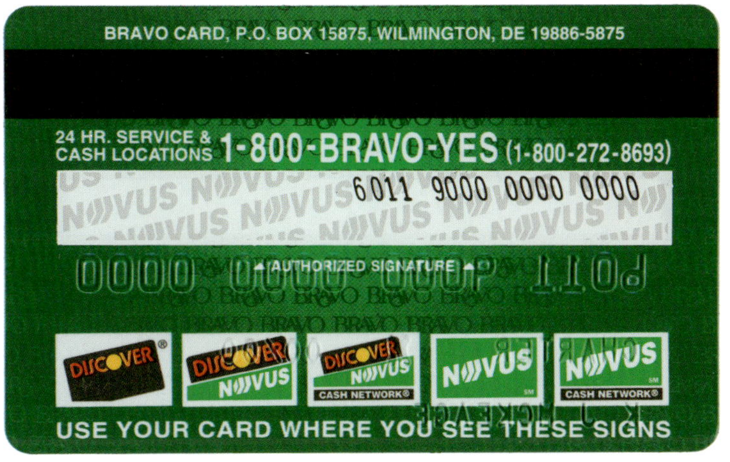

Figure 46.
BRAVO credit card, United States, 1996. Donated by Discover Corporation.

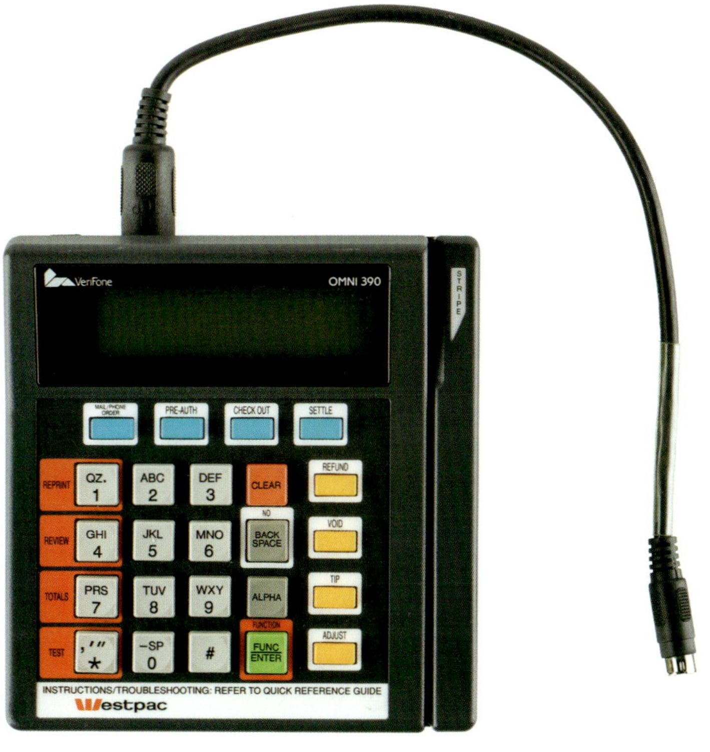

Figure 47.
VeriFone credit card reader, United States, late 1990s. Donated by MasterCard International Inc.

Consumer Credit and Popular Culture

Companies often advertise which credit cards they accept but do not mention cash. A *New Yorker* cartoon (Figure 48) from 1964 entitled "Do You Accept Cash?" mocks how, with the growing popularity of credit cards, consumers may be uncertain as to whether or not vendors would accept cash as a valid form of payment.

Figure 48.
"Do You Accept Cash?" cartoon, The New Yorker, *1964. James Mulligan/The New Yorker Collection/The Cartoon Bank. Donated by Alfred Bloomingdale.*

DIGITAL TRANSACTIONS

Mobile Money Systems and Developing Economies

With the absence of widespread banking infrastructure and internet access in countries with developing economies, mobile money offers the first real alternative to using physical currencies to make transactions. Mobile money systems allow users to visit a store or kiosk and deposit cash into a unique account accessed via cell phone (Figures 49–51). Once cash is deposited, customers can make payments to individuals and businesses through their phone network, avoiding the need to carry cash or to have access to a bank account. Mobile money was first developed in Kenya in 2007 under the name M-Pesa. The *M* stands for mobile, and *pesa* is a word for money in Kiswahili, a language spoken in Kenya.

Figure 49.
Mobile phone, Kenya, 2014.
Donated by Gregory Deacon.

Figure 50.
Subscriber identity module (SIM) card, Kenya, 2014. Donated by Gregory Deacon.

Figure 51.
Kiosk manager with kiosk used for cash deposits to mobile money systems in Nairobi, Kenya. Photo courtesy of Jennifer Huxta.

Cryptocurrencies

Cryptocurrencies are not issued by a government or single authority; instead, they are generated by a computer protocol and rely on an electronic peer-to-peer system of exchange. Their value comes from the mutual agreement of their users and their limited supply. The first cryptocurrency, Bitcoin, emerged in 2009 and has received the most attention from the media (Figure 52). Many other cryptocurrencies have been established since.

Figure 52.
Bitcoin Magazine, *United States, 2014. Donated by Alexander K. Dewar.*

Payment Dongles for Smartphones and Tablets

Electronic devices called payment dongles, such as the Square Reader, enable individuals and small businesses to accept payments from credit and debit cards via applications on smartphones and tablets (Figures 53 and 54). The dongle reads the magnetic stripes on credit and debit cards, and the application keeps a record of transactions. Payment dongles transform smartphones and tablets into portable cash registers.

Figure 53.
Square Reader, United States, 2013.
Donated by Square, Inc.

Figure 54.
Mobile phone, United States, 2012.
Donated by Hillery L. York and Nicholas W. Dikker.

NEW BANKNOTE SECURITY FEATURES AND DESIGNS

Polymer Banknotes

More than thirty countries around the world have replaced some of their paper notes with plastic notes, called polymer notes. Polymer notes were first issued in Australia in 1988 and are believed to be more durable and more difficult to counterfeit than paper notes (Figure 55). These notes include new security features, such as embedded clear lenses, that are difficult to imitate and cannot be achieved with paper notes.

Figure 55.
Ten dollar note, Australia, 1988.
Donated by Andrew Shiva.

The New U.S. 100 Dollar Bill

In 2013, the U.S. government released a redesigned 100 dollar note made from paper with enhanced security features, including a 3D blue security ribbon and a color-changing image of a bell, as well as new artwork on the reverse (Figure 56). With these changes, the 100 dollar note is more colorful and complex than its predecessor (Figure 57).

Figure 56.
One hundred dollar note, United States, 2013.

Figure 57.
One hundred dollar note, United States, 1996.

NEW NATIONAL AND REGIONAL CURRENCIES

Money and Nationhood

Despite the growth of cashless payment systems and worldwide acceptance of major currencies, such as the U.S. dollar and the euro, the currencies of smaller nations remain a strong symbol and signal of statehood. As new nations emerge, some choose to issue their own national currencies rather than adopt a major world currency. The world's youngest country, the Republic of South Sudan, created the South Sudanese pound in 2011, the same year it became a nation (Figures 58 and 59).

Figure 58.
Five pound note, South Sudan, 2011. Donated by Zoe Cormack.

Figure 59.
The Republic of South Sudan is located in eastern Africa.

New National Currencies

The breakup of Yugoslavia during the early 1990s led to the creation of five new national currencies in Slovenia, Croatia, Bosnia and Herzegovina, Macedonia, and Serbia. Around the same time, the African nation of Eritrea became independent from Ethiopia and issued its own national currency, the nakfa. New national currencies often contain images emphasizing national sovereignty, such as the depiction of the raising of the national flag on the nakfa (Figure 60).

Figure 60.
Ten nakfa note, Eritrea, 2012.
Donated by Awet T. Weldemichael.

The Euro

The euro began to circulate in 2002, replacing the national currencies of many European nations. The establishment of this regional currency reflects a movement in Europe toward integration and a willingness to place trust in a shared monetary system. Each nation that has adopted the euro is allowed to decorate the reverse of some coins with national symbols or designs (Figure 61). Euro notes depict windows and bridges that reflect seven European architectural styles but do not contain nation-specific designs (Figure 62).

Figure 61.
One euro coin, Netherlands, 2000. Donated by Alexander K. Dewar.

Figure 62.
Five euro note, European Union, 2013. Donated by Alexander K. Dewar.

European Currencies before the Euro

Before the euro, European nations each had their own national currencies, such as Belgian francs, Greek drachmas, and Italian lire (Figures 63 and 64). Given recent instability with the euro, some question whether this regional currency will survive or if European nations will eventually decide to issue their own national currencies once again.

Figure 63.
One hundred franc note, Belgium, 1978–1981. Donated by Christine Y. Ferdinand and Russell D. Feingold.

Figure 64.
One hundred drachma note, Greece, 1978. Donated by Christine Y. Ferdinand and Russell D. Feingold.

THE MESSAGES OF MONEY

Money talks.
—Unknown

The most prominent message on money is often the denomination, or monetary value, but it is rarely the only message. Through images and text, governments use money to make both subtle and overt political and cultural statements about a nation's identity, leadership, heritage, and values. The practice of attaching messages to money makes coins and notes valuable sources for learning about global cultures and history.

American money in the eighteenth and nineteenth centuries contained a wide range of political messages relating to the young nation. Notes and coins depicted symbols and scenes that portrayed and reinforced democratic principles and national unity. Some concepts were expressed through imagery and classical allegory. The personification of Justice is portrayed on a fifty dollar interest-bearing note from 1863 as a woman holding scales. The idea of unity among the thirteen colonies is conveyed on a one-sixth dollar note from the Pennsylvania Colony through the depiction of thirteen interlocking rings. Other messages were more direct, such as the phrase "'Tis Death to Counterfeit," which appeared on many colonial notes to notify users of the strict punishment for violating the law.

The inclusion of portraits of national icons on money can be traced back thousands of years to ancient political figures, such as the emperors of Rome. The widespread practice of depicting national leaders on money makes coins particularly robust sources for studying the succession of governments and the ways in which rulers communicated and demonstrated authority. American money has featured—and continues to feature—many of the nation's founding fathers and leading political figures, such as George Washington, James Madison, and Abraham Lincoln. Their portraits invoke a feeling of stability and continuity, reminding people of the nation's strong leadership through times of crisis and discord.

National icons and political messages are often portrayed alongside cultural messages, which can reflect or even help shape a community's identity. For example, the inclusion of multiple languages on money can convey existing linguistic diversity, such as the seventeen languages on Indian rupee notes, or can spread the acceptance of a new language or script. Religious messages on money can highlight a widely held belief, introduce a new religious doctrine, or, as with the American motto "In God we trust," connect the fate of the nation to the will of the divine. The use of imagery of historic sites, such as the pyramids of Egypt, can be employed by governments to promote their ideas about national heritage, identity, and tradition.

In addition to the messages that appear on money, monetary objects created for special circumstances convey information about their times and places simply through their creation and use. For example, the introduction of separate currencies for persecuted people, such as notes issued to Jewish people in Nazi concentration camps and Jewish ghettos during the Holocaust, reveal not only a little-understood aspect of the history of that genocide but also the ways in which money can be used as a social and political device of oppression. Special currencies have also been created during times of economic difficulty; hard-times tokens produced in the 1830s reflect coin shortages in America; food stamps are a sign of hardship and hunger as well as the U.S. government's response to poverty.

By attaching messages to money, governments have revealed much about the ways in which leaders saw themselves, how they wanted their citizens and subjects to see them, and how they treated the people whose lives and well-being relied on the money they issued.

Unity

During the Revolutionary period, American money often contained messages about unity. The image of thirteen interlocking rings on continental notes was intended to illustrate the solidarity of the thirteen colonies against the British Crown (Figure 65). In the 1780s, the new national motto, "E Pluribus Unum"—or "out of many, one"—began to appear on American coins (Figure 66).

Figure 65.
One-sixth dollar note, Pennsylvania Colony, 1776. Donated by the Stack family.

Figure 66.
One cent coin, New Jersey Colony, 1786. Donated by J. G. Bruff.

Independence and Strength

Some Continental currency of the Revolutionary period contained graphic illustrations inspired by the American colonies fighting and defeating Great Britain. One example is South Carolina Colony's seventy dollar note from 1779 (Figure 67), in which America is depicted as an eagle eating the liver of the Greek god Prometheus, who represents a chained Great Britain.[1] The eagle has become a prominent symbol of national strength on American money (Figure 68).

Figure 67.
Seventy dollar note, South Carolina Colony, 1779.

Figure 68.
Five thousand dollar proof legal tender note, United States, 1878.

Liberty and Justice

Political ideals and values, such as liberty and justice, have often been depicted on American money as allegorical figures. On the interest-bearing note of 1863, Justice is shown holding her scales (Figure 69). A strong Liberty with her sword and shield appears on the right side of the fifty dollar note from 1880 (Figure 70). Liberty has also appeared on many U.S. coins.

Figure 69.
Fifty dollar interest-bearing note, United States, 1863. Donated by the Stack family.

Figure 70.
Fifty dollar legal tender note, United States, 1880. Donated by U.S. Department of the Treasury.

The Rule of Law

Currency issued by governments is protected by law. Historically, money has conveyed messages to people about the consequences of counterfeiting it. Many American colonial notes from the 1770s (Figure 71) plainly state the punishment for falsely imitating the legal tender at the time, with phrases like "'Tis Death to Counterfeit."

Figure 71.
Thirty shilling note, New Jersey Colony, 1776.

Counterfeiting Money

Counterfeiting money is illegal. It threatens an economy because it may prompt people to question if their money is genuine and if it will be accepted as payment. Governments also seek to prevent counterfeiting because it threatens their authority to manufacture money and to determine what can be used as legal tender. The presence of counterfeits may indicate that people lack confidence in a government or respect for its authority (Figure 72).

Figure 72.
Counterfeit twenty dollar legal tender note, United States, circa 1862. Donated by The Chase Manhattan Bank.

Foreign Coinage in Colonial America

The American colonies faced a persistent problem of coin shortages due in part to Great Britain's restrictions on the importation of coins. Colonists relied on any currency they could find, which included a wide range of coins from Great Britain, France, the Netherlands, Italy, Germany, and Spain (Figures 73a–73b).[2] The most common coin was the silver eight real, also known as a Spanish piece of eight. The Spanish minted these coins from silver mined in their colonies in the Americas. Pieces of eight were not only widespread in the Americas but also circulated in Europe, Asia, and Africa, making the coin the world's first global currency.[3] Colonists also cut pieces from these and other coins to make smaller denominations (Figure 74). The use of foreign coins reflects some of the economic and political challenges colonists faced prior to the Revolutionary War and highlights how economic hardship and global interactions helped stimulate political movements for independence.

Figure 73a.
Eight real coin, Bolivia, 1681.
Donated by the Stack family.

Figure 73b.
Eight real coin, Mexico, 1762.

Figure 74.
Portion of a real coin, Curacao, 1819–1825.

Money Made by American Colonists

Shortages of coins in colonial America motivated colonists to mint and print their own money. In 1652, the Massachusetts Colony produced the first colonial American coins, and in 1690, it issued the first colonial paper money (Figures 75–77). Colonists' creation of currencies demonstrated their increasing autonomy from Great Britain.

Figure 75. New England shilling coin, Massachusetts Colony, 1652. Donated by Emery May Holden Norweb.

Figure 76. Pine tree shilling coin, Massachusetts Colony, 1667–1674. Donated by Emery May Holden Norweb.

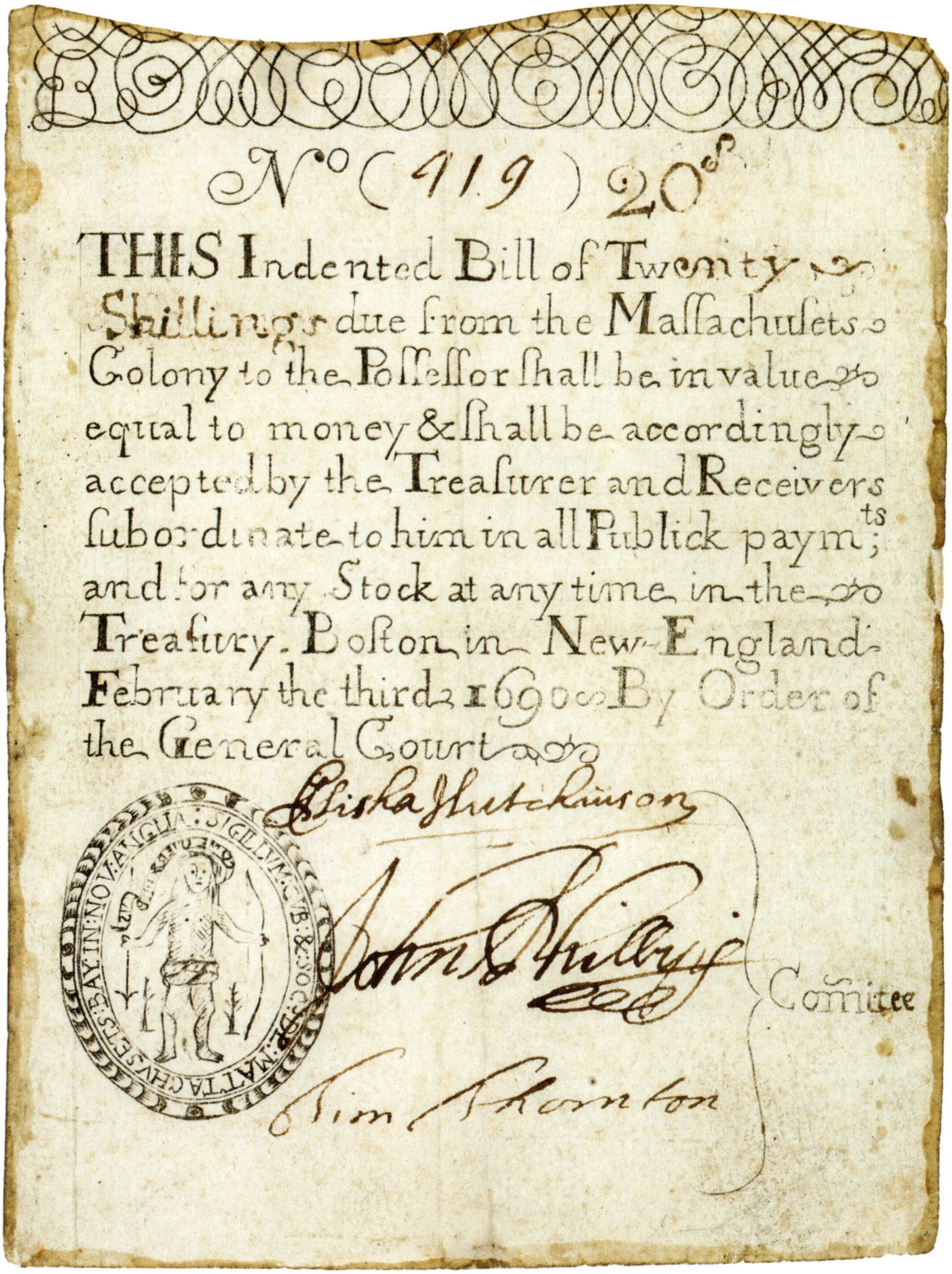

No (419) 20s

THIS Indented Bill of Twenty Shillings due from the Massachusets Colony to the Possessor shall be in value equal to money & shall be accordingly accepted by the Treasurer and Receivers subordinate to him in all Publick paymts; and for any Stock at any time in the Treasury. Boston in New-England February the third 1690 By Order of the General Court

Elisha Hutchinson

John Phillips

Tim Thornton

Comitee

Figure 77.
Altered twenty shilling note,
Massachusetts Colony, 1690–1691.

Notes of the Civil War Era

At the beginning of the Civil War the U.S. government issued federal notes, often called greenbacks, to finance its war efforts (Figures 78 and 79). The government of the Confederate States of America also issued its own paper money depicting Confederate leadership and scenes from life in the South, including images of slavery (Figure 80). The difference in political messages on the notes reflects the division between the northern and southern regions of the United States during the Civil War.

Figure 78.
Five dollar demand note, United States, 1861. Donated by Roland S. Wilson.

Figure 79.
Five dollar demand note, United States, 1861. Donated by Roland S. Wilson.

Figure 80.
Ten dollar note, Confederate States of America, 1861. Donated by Woodbury S. Ober.

NATIONAL ICONS

George Washington

The depiction of the first U.S. president, George Washington, on money has changed dramatically over the last two centuries. In early appearances, Washington was depicted crowned with a laurel wreath, like the emperors of ancient Rome, and in a toga like a mythological god (Figures 81–83). Over time, his look became less regal, increasingly reflecting the democratic role of the presidency (Figure 84).

Figure 81.
Sestertius coin, Roman Empire, 98–117 CE.

Figure 82.
One cent coin, United States, 1783.

Figure 83.
Three dollar note, United States, nineteenth century. Donated by Richard S. Schlein.

Figure 84.
One dollar silver certificate, United States, 1923.

James Madison

James Madison was the fourth U.S. president and is often referred to as the "Father of the Constitution" because of his role in writing America's founding documents. His portrait has been featured on the 5,000 dollar denominations of multiple series of U.S. notes (Figure 85). His signature is visible on a personal check he wrote in 1813 (Figure 86).

Figure 85.
Five thousand dollar Federal Reserve note, United States, 1928. Donated by U.S. Department of the Treasury.

Figure 86.
A personal check of James Madison for 69.70 dollars, United States, 1813.

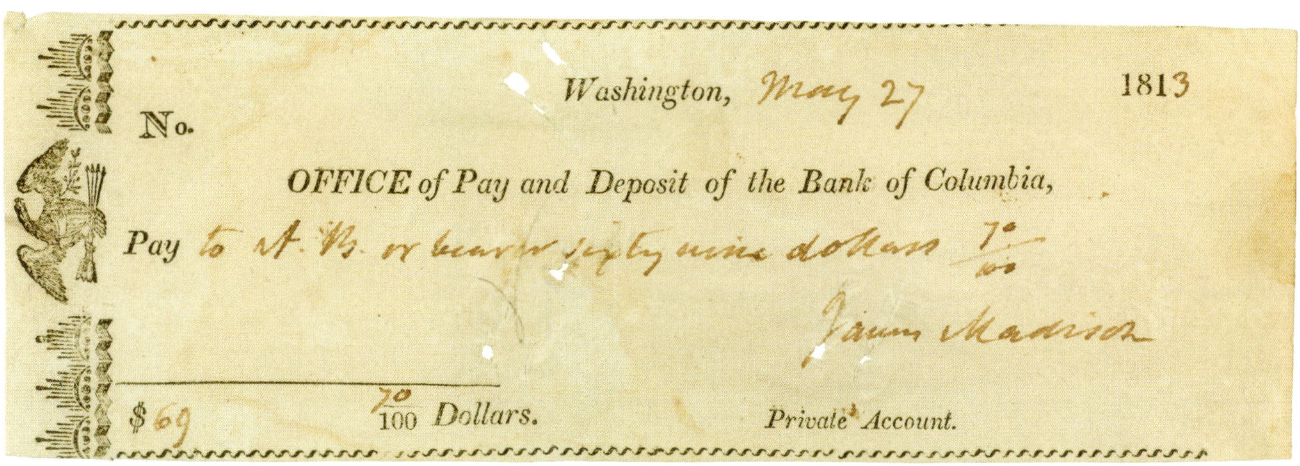

Abraham Lincoln

President Abraham Lincoln was the first historic figure to be depicted on a circulating coin issued by the U.S. Mint. The decision to include him on the 1909 cent designed by Victor D. Brenner reflects his position as a symbol of national unity and stability (Figures 87 and 88). Lincoln has also been featured on U.S. paper money (Figure 89).

Figure 87.
One cent coin, United States, 1909. Donated by Frederic A. Delano.

Figure 88.
Abraham Lincoln plaque by Victor D. Brenner, United States, circa 1907. Donated by U.S. Department of the Treasury.

Figure 89.
Five hundred dollar gold certificate, United States, 1922. Donated by U.S. Department of the Treasury.

Language and Multiculturalism

The languages used on money convey a message about the community for which the currency is intended. Among the earliest bilingual coins are the Indo-Greek drachms from about 160 BCE in modern Afghanistan and Pakistan. They feature both Greek and the Kharoshthi script, used to write an Indian language (Figure 90). This reflects the ethnic and cultural diversity in the region. Many modern notes feature multiple languages and more than one script, such as the 500 ruble note from the Republic of Azerbaijan, which has Latin, Cyrillic, and Arabic script (Figure 91).

Figure 90.
Drachm coin, Bactria, circa 160 BCE. Donated by Raymond and Meryem Hebert.

Figure 91.
Five hundred ruble note, Republic of Azerbaijan, 1920. Donated by The Chase Manhattan Bank.

Multilingualism and American Coinage: The Peso Cent Sketch

The United States took over Puerto Rico during the Spanish–American War in 1898. The peso cent sketch (Figure 92) drawn by U.S. Mint engraver Charles E. Barber indicates that the United States may have considered issuing a peso coin worth sixty cents in 1899 for the "Isla de Puerto Rico." The coin was never issued, but the sketch is a reminder of the long history of multilingualism in America and the significance of the choice of language on money.

Figure 92.
Peso cent sketch, United States, 1899.
Donated by the Stack family.

Religious Messages

Money has often been used to carry religious messages. The United States first included "In God We Trust" on circulating coins in 1864 (Figure 93). The inclusion of religious messages was also widespread in the Islamic world. From the seventh to the nineteenth century, many Islamic coins stated versions of the Profession of Faith—"There is no God but God alone"—and religious verses from the Quran (Figures 94 and 95).

Figure 93.
One dollar coin, United States, 1921. Donated by Jeff Garrett.

Figure 94.
Dinar coin, Umayyad dynasty–ruled Middle East, 713–714 CE.

Figure 95.
Dirhem coin, Damascus (Syria), 698–699 CE. Donated by Raymond and Meryem Hebert.

Goddess Juno Moneta

The word *money* is derived from the Roman goddess Juno Moneta. She did not represent money to ancient Romans; rather, her name meant "she who warns."[4] She became associated with money because coins were minted in her temple in Rome. Over time, *moneta* came to be used to refer to places where coins were made and eventually to money itself. Juno Moneta is depicted on this Roman denarius coin from the first century BCE (Figure 96).

Figure 96.
Denarius coin, Roman Republic, 46 BCE. Donated by The Chase Manhattan Bank.

Cultural Heritage

Many nations use money to reflect and define their cultural heritage. Notes from Egypt, for example, feature the pyramids, hieroglyphics, and ancient sculpture. Similarly, Chinese notes depict the Great Wall of China, and colonial notes for the British Mandate for Palestine are decorated with monuments of the Old City of Jerusalem (Figure 97).

Figure 97.
Five hundred mil note, British Mandate for Palestine, 1927.
Donated by Catherine Bullowa.

MESSAGES OF CIRCUMSTANCE

Persecution and Genocide

During the Holocaust, Nazi officials created notes for use by Jewish people in concentration camps and ghettos. Jewish people were forced to exchange national currencies for camp and ghetto money, which had limited or no value inside specific places of Nazi imprisonment and served as a device to deceive, isolate, denationalize, and steal from Jewish people.[5] Many ghetto and concentration camp currencies feature Jewish symbols, such as the Star of David, and some bear signatures of Jewish leaders of specific communities to associate the currency with the people who were forced to use it. The use and circulation of these currencies varied by location; the notes issued for the Łódź ghetto in Poland (Figure 98) could be used to make limited purchases inside the ghetto, whereas the notes created for the Theresienstadt ghetto (Figure 99) in Czechoslovakia supported a Nazi propaganda campaign intended to make the ghetto appear humane to international visitors and organizations, such as the Red Cross.[6] Survivors of Theresienstadt recall that they relied on special coupons, rather than these notes, to obtain essential items, such as food and clothing.

Figure 98.
Fifty pfennig note, Łódź ghetto and labor camp in Poland, 1940. Donated by the Stack family.

Figure 99.
One hundred kronen note, Theresienstadt ghetto and concentration camp in Czechoslovakia, 1943.

Wartime Emergencies and Imprisonment

Emergency currencies have often been issued during wartime. After the Japanese bombing of Pearl Harbor in 1941, the United States withdrew its regular notes from Hawaii and issued notes printed with the island's name to protect the national currency in case Hawaii fell to Japanese invasion (Figure 100). Armies also issued currencies specifically for prisoners of war (Figure 101).

Figure 100.
Five dollar "Hawaii" Federal Reserve note, United States, circa 1942. Donated by Mrs. F. C. C. Boyd.

Figure 101.
Fifty centime coupon, France, 1914–1919.

Military Occupancy

The currencies in Figures 102 and 103 were issued by Allied governments during and immediately after the Second World War. The lira and mark notes are called Allied Military Currencies and were used by both military officials and civilians in newly occupied areas to protect Allied national currencies from inflation. The British government also issued Armed Forces Special Vouchers in an attempt to prevent military goods from being sold on the postwar black market.

Figure 102.
One lira Allied Military note, Italy, 1943. Donated by Mr. and Mrs. Mortimer L. Neinken.

Figure 103.
One thousand mark Allied Military note, Germany, 1944.

Currency Shortages

During the 1830s and the early 1840s, the United States faced economic decline and a shortage of coins. Copper tokens, called hard-times tokens, were issued privately and used as money. Some contain satirical images, such as a tortoise carrying a safe with the word "Treasury" on it (Figure 104).[7]

Figure 104.
Hard-times token, United States, 1837. Donated by Mendel L. Peterson.

Hardship and Hunger

Food stamps are issued by the U.S. government to low-income families and individuals and are accepted by most grocery stores as money for food purchases. The United States first began issuing food stamps in 1939 to help struggling families during the Great Depression. Since then, the government has also developed special programs for mothers and babies in need (Figure 105).

Figure 105.
Food certificate, United States, circa 1970. Donated by U.S. Department of Agriculture.

Taxation: The Beard Token

In the late seventeenth century, Russian Emperor Peter I instituted a tax on beards because he regarded them as in poor taste when compared with modern fashions in Europe. Any man who wanted to keep his beard was forced to pay a tax and carry a token (Figure 106). The token depicts a beard and mustache.

Figure 106.
Beard token, Russia, 1705. Donated by Willis H. du Pont.

THE ARTISTRY OF MONEY

The aim of art is to represent not the outward appearance of things, but their inward significance.
—Will Durant, American philosopher[1]

Coins and notes do not have to be beautiful to serve as money, but they have often featured purposeful and symbolic art. Creative design and skill have been applied to the production of money to honor people, commemorate significant events, and inspire respect and loyalty to governments. Thus, the art of money is not only in its design but also in the way in which numismatic artwork can convey the importance of money in society and its power as a means of communication for governments and artists.

Coins have been used as a canvas for artwork for millennia. Ancient Greek coins featured ethereal deities, attractive symbols, and strong leaders in high relief. The beauty of ancient coins has served as inspiration for many modern designs, including some of America's most iconic: the ten and twenty dollar gold coins first issued in 1907. Celebrated sculptor Augustus Saint-Gaudens crafted the design for these coins at the request of President Theodore Roosevelt, who was unimpressed with the look of American coins at the turn of the century. The partnership between the sculptor and the president harnessed the artistry of classical sculpture while celebrating American symbols, like Lady Liberty and the eagle. The result was a design that, when realized in ultra high relief as Saint-Gaudens intended, appears more like a miniature sculpture than a modern coin. Like Saint-Gaudens, many of the artists responsible for America's coins, such as George T. Morgan and Victor D. Brenner, have also created artwork on a larger scale in the form of sculptures, art medals, and plaques.

The design of paper money is driven by the need to make notes difficult to forge in order to prevent counterfeiting, yet notes feature artwork that is not only complex but also striking and representational. Existing works of art can be a source of inspiration for the designs on paper money. For example, the 1863 series of national bank notes depicts the historic paintings that hang in the U.S. Capitol Rotunda. Delicately engraved, the national bank notes are impressive replications of the original large-scale artwork. The scenes they depict, such as the signing of the Declaration of Independence and the embarkation of the pilgrims on their journey to America, convey key patriotic moments for Americans. They also showcase the artistic skill of the engravers who reduced the paintings to a fraction of their original size while maintaining their quality and essence.

The creation of a new note series can also be the impetus for the development of original artwork. One of the finest examples of this is the 1896 series of U.S. silver certificates. The designs for this series were developed by artists commissioned by the Bureau of Engraving and Printing, all of whom trained as muralists.[2] The notes are often regarded as the most beautiful American notes ever made, featuring stunning neoclassical designs with allegorical scenes on the reverse and significant figures, such as Samuel Morse and Martha Washington, on the obverse.

When money is produced, it carries an official design, but once it is released to the public, it can be used as a medium for unofficial artistic and personal expression. Notes can be turned into pulp, a material that can be used to create sculptures much like papier-mâché. They can also be altered with a pen and often depict national leaders, making them an easy target for satire and unconventional political messaging. The portability and malleability of coins make them an appealing medium for the creation of mementos. People can engrave coins to feature characters and personal messages or elongate them to obscure the original design and replace it with an image, turning what was once money into a souvenir of a place or experience. Both altered and unaltered coins can be pierced to make them into pendants or can be fused with other materials to create jewelry and ornaments. The creation of art from money destroys its monetary value but often enhances its personal and sentimental value.

The deliberate creation of artwork for coins and notes—and from coins and notes—makes them ideal objects for exploring how national symbols, artistic ideals and practices, and production technologies have changed over time and vary across the globe.

The Master Die Engravers of Ancient Sicily

The coins in Figures 107 and 108 were struck with dies made by master engravers from the ancient Greek city of Syracuse on the island of Sicily during the fifth century BCE. They are generally regarded as masterpieces of Greek art, and their engravers are considered some of the most accomplished artists of the time. Some engravers were so proud of their dies that they signed them, claiming their work for eternity. The ancient artist Kimon engraved the die used to make the decadrachm coin in Figure 108. He signed his work with his initial K, placing it on the crown on the goddess Arethusa's head.

Figure 107.
Decadrachm coin, Syracuse, Sicily, 465 BCE. Donated by John Whitney Walter.

Figure 108.
Decadrachm of Syracuse, signed by Kimon, circa 405–400 BCE. *Struck, silver; 43.3 g. Harvard Art Museums/Arthur M. Sackler Museum, loan from the Trustees of the Arthur Stone Dewing Greek Numismatic Foundation, 1.1965.869. Photo courtesy of Imaging Department © President and Fellows of Harvard College.*

Inspiring American Coin Design

President Theodore Roosevelt was inspired by the artistic merit of ancient coins and sought to change the look of American coinage (Figure 109).[3] In 1905, he asked famous sculptor Augustus Saint-Gaudens to create new designs for the U.S. cent, ten dollar, and twenty dollar coins, taking his inspiration from the high relief and fine quality of ancient coins (Figure 110).[4]

Figure 109.
Theodore Roosevelt inaugural medal by Augustus Saint-Gaudens, United States, 1905.

Figure 110.
Tetradrachm coin, Macedon, 336–323 BCE.

Augustus Saint-Gaudens

Augustus Saint-Gaudens began working to redesign American coinage in 1905 (Figure 111). He created innovative new designs for the ten and twenty dollar gold coins but faced strong opposition from the U.S. Mint, whose officials encountered significant challenges in the production of Saint-Gaudens' high relief designs.[5]

Figure 111.
Augustus Saint-Gaudens at work in his studio. Photo courtesy of U.S. Department of the Interior, National Park Service, Saint-Gaudens National Historic Site, Cornish, New Hampshire.

Saint-Gaudens' Eagles

In 1907, the ten and twenty dollar gold coins designed by Augustus Saint-Gaudens were released to the public and were immediately in high demand (Figures 112 and 113). The twenty dollar coin, also called a double eagle, is widely considered the most beautiful American coin ever made for circulation. Saint-Gaudens' design was last used on a coin of this denomination in 1933, as the U.S. government ended the circulation of gold coins the following year.

Figure 112.
Twenty dollar "Double Eagle" coin, United States, 1907. Donated by F. A. Hauck.

Figure 113.
Ten dollar "Eagle" coin, United States, 1907. Donated by Estate of Josiah K. Lilly Jr.

Realizing Saint-Gaudens' Double Eagle

Augustus Saint-Gaudens' design for the twenty dollar gold coin was ahead of its time. His ultra high relief design could not be fully realized by the U.S. Mint, so it was altered in order to produce coins for circulation in 1907. About a century later, the U.S. Mint revisited Saint-Gaudens' ambitious design, digitally mapping his coin plasters and employing new minting technologies to fully implement his plans. The result was a commemorative coin that reveals the full beauty of Saint-Gaudens' artistic vision (Figure 114). It represents how new technologies can lead to more advanced coin designs.

Figure 114.
Twenty dollar "Double Eagle" commemorative coin, United States, 2009. Transfer from U.S. Mint.

Glenna Goodacre's Sacagawea Dollar

In 1997, the U.S. Mint initiated a search for a design for the obverse of the millennium golden dollar. American sculptor Glenna Goodacre's design depicts a Native American woman named Sacagawea, who accompanied American explorers Meriwether Lewis and William Clark on their journey to the western United States (Figures 115 and 116). Sacagawea is one of only three historic women depicted on American coins.

Figure 115.
Coin plaster, United States, 1998.
Donated by Glenna Goodacre.

Figure 116.
One dollar, United States, 2000.
Transfer from U.S. Mint.

MEDALS AND PLAQUES BY COIN ARTISTS: MORGAN, SAINT-GAUDENS, AND BRENNER

Sculptors are often commissioned to design and engrave coin dies. The medals and plaques in Figures 117–119 were made by three artists: George T. Morgan, Augustus Saint-Gaudens, and Victor D. Brenner. They are each responsible for some of America's most famous coin designs. These works of art showcase the artists' talents on a larger scale.

Figure 117.
Theodore Roosevelt plaque by George T. Morgan, United States, early twentieth century.

Figure 118.
Colombian Exposition medal by Augustus Saint-Gaudens and Charles E. Barber, United States, 1892–1893. Donated by Frederic A. Delano.

Figure 119.
Motherhood medal by Victor D. Brenner, United States, 1909. Donated by Frederic A. Delano.

Converting Art into Currency

In 1863, the United States issued its first national bank notes and decided to feature historically themed paintings from the U.S. Capitol Rotunda on the reverse (Figure 120). Engravers depicted the paintings at reduced size—from the original 12 × 8 feet to a mere 4.5 × 2.5 inches—while maintaining the paintings' detail and quality. This decision converted national treasures into national currency.

Figure 120.
The paintings of the U.S. Capitol Rotunda in situ. Photo courtesy of Architect of the Capitol.

Vanderlyn's Painting on the Five Dollar Note

John Vanderlyn's painting of Italian explorer Christopher Columbus was installed in the U.S. Capitol Rotunda in 1847. It depicts the landing of Columbus on a beach in the West Indies in 1492 (Figure 121). This moment is often regarded as the beginning of European engagement with the Americas. The painting was replicated on the first five dollar national bank note (Figure 122).

Figure 121.
Landing of Columbus *by John Vanderlyn. Photo courtesy of Architect of the Capitol.*

Figure 122.
Five dollar proof national bank note, United States, circa 1863.

Weir's Painting on the Fifty Dollar Note

Robert Walter Weir completed *Embarkation of the Pilgrims* in 1843. The painting depicts the Pilgrims departing Holland in 1620 in search of religious freedom in America (Figure 123). The painting conveys the solemnity of the travelers at the beginning of their journey. Weir's painting is replicated on the reverse of the first fifty dollar national bank note (Figure 124).

Figure 123.
Embarkation of the Pilgrims *by Robert Walter Weir. Photo courtesy of Architect of the Capitol.*

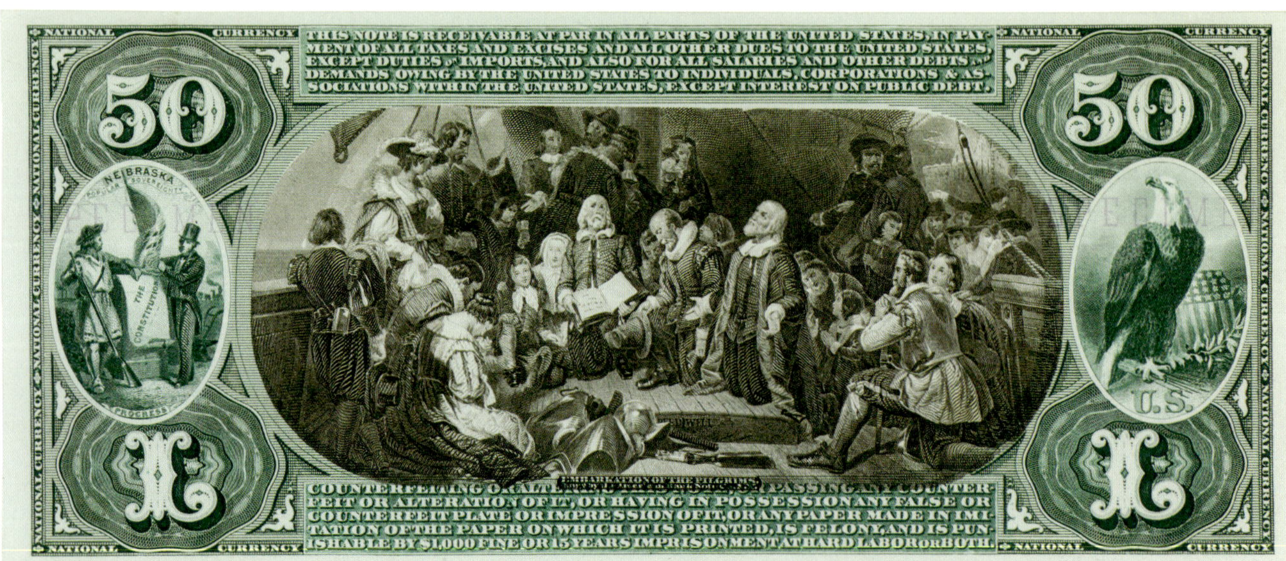

Figure 124.
Fifty dollar proof national bank note, United States, circa 1863.

Trumbull's Paintings on the 100 Dollar and 500 Dollar Notes

John Trumbull painted four of the eight paintings in the U.S. Capitol Rotunda. His paintings *Declaration of Independence* and *Surrender of General Burgoyne* are featured on the reverse of the first 100 dollar and 500 dollar national bank notes (Figures 125–128).

Figure 125.
Declaration of Independence *by John Trumbull. Photo courtesy of Architect of the Capitol.*

Figure 126.
One hundred dollar proof national bank note, United States, circa 1863.

Figure 127.
Surrender of General Burgoyne *by John Trumbull. Photo courtesy of Architect of the Capitol.*

Figure 128.
Five hundred dollar national bank note, United States, circa 1865.

1896 U.S. Educational Note Series

The U.S. government released a series of silver certificates in 1896 with neoclassical designs. They are considered to be among the most beautiful American notes ever printed. These notes are often referred to as the "Educational Series." The one dollar note depicts the allegorical figure of History instructing Youth (Figure 129). The two dollar note depicts the figure of Science presenting the children, Steam and Electricity, to the adults, Commerce and Manufacture (Figure 130). The figure of Electricity also appears on the five dollar note, but there she has matured into a powerful woman of influence (Figure 131).

Figure 129.
One dollar silver certificate, United States, 1896. Donated by U.S. Department of the Treasury.

Figure 130.
Two dollar silver certificate, United States, 1896. Donated by U.S. Department of the Treasury.

Figure 131.
Five dollar silver certificate, United States, 1896. Donated by U.S. Department of the Treasury.

The Design of the U.S. Dollar

The design of the U.S. one dollar note has not changed since 1963. Today's one dollar note features the first U.S. president, George Washington, on the obverse and the Great Seal of the United States on the reverse (Figure 132). The Great Seal design contains many significant symbols. The bald eagle represents the nation. The eagle holds arrows in one talon and an olive branch in the other, signifying war and peace. On the eagle's breast is a shield with thirteen stripes, one for each American colony. Opposite the eagle is a pyramid in thirteen levels topped with an all-seeing eye. Inscribed at the pyramid's base in Roman numerals is 1776, the year the Declaration of Independence was adopted.

*Figure 132.
One dollar note, United States, 2009. Donated by Chester T. Dussault and Susan L. Feingold.*

Macerated-Note Sculptures

The busts of American presidents George Washington and Abraham Lincoln shown in Figures 133 and 134 are made from notes. The notes were macerated, that is, soaked in water to break them down and then converted into pulp. The remaining material was then transformed into sculpture, similar to papier-mâché artwork. Fragments of the designs of national notes are visible on Lincoln's neck.

Figure 133.
Abraham Lincoln macerated-note sculpture, United States, nineteenth to twentieth century. Donated by Abraham Goldstein.

Figure 134.
George Washington macerated-note sculpture, United States, nineteenth to twentieth century. Donated by the Stack family.

Sketching Satire

Portraits on paper notes are easy targets for satire. Figure 135 shows an example of fractional currency, paper notes worth less than one dollar, featuring the portrait of William M. Meredith, secretary of the U.S. Treasury from 1849 to 1850. With ink pen, satirists have transformed Meredith into less dignified figures, including a pirate and a musician, in Figures 136 and 137.

Figure 135.
Ten cent note, United States, 1874.
Donated by H. K. Crofoot.

Figure 136.
Modified ten cent note, United States, circa 1874. Donated by The Chase Manhattan Bank.

Figure 137.
Modified ten cent note, United States, circa 1874. Donated by The Chase Manhattan Bank.

Modified Coins

The individuals depicted on American coins are carefully selected, and their portraits are designed under the supervision of U.S. Mint officials. Once these coins enter circulation, however, they can be altered to feature alternative designs. U.S. nickels have often been targeted for modification due to their size and the malleability of their metal. The artfully modified coins are often referred to as "hobo nickels" because they are inexpensive and portable (Figure 138).

Figure 138.
Modified coin, United States, early twenty-first century. Donated by Jay L. DeBoer.

Elongated Coins

Coins can be stretched and imprinted with designs to make souvenirs or tokens. The first elongated coins are thought to have been made at the Columbian Exposition, also called the World's Fair of 1893 (Figure 139). By 1933, visitors to the World's Fair in Chicago could make elongated coins to commemorate their visits to various venues, such as the Planetarium or the Streets of Paris (Figure 140). Elongated coins are still a popular souvenir today.

Figure 139.
Columbian Exposition elongated coin, United States, 1893. Donated by Lonnie Mimms.

Figure 140.
Streets of Paris elongated coin, United States, 1933. Donated by Edith R. Meggers.

Love Tokens

These coins are called love tokens because their official markings have been replaced with personal messages. Some have artistically arranged initials, and others depict objects of personal significance, as in the 1876 U.S. quarter engraved with an image of the Bible shown in Figure 141. Because love tokens are engraved by hand, they are unique. They may be used as lucky charms, jewelry, or commemorative gifts (Figures 142 and 143).

Figure 141.
Love token, United States, nineteenth century. Donated by Mendel L. Peterson.

Figure 142.
Love token brooch, United States, circa 1880. Donated by Mendel L. Peterson.

Figure 143.
Love token, United States, nineteenth century.

Jewelry Made from Coins

Gold and silver have been used for both coinage and jewelry for more than 2,600 years. Coins intended for circulation as money have also been paired with precious gemstones and other metals to make jewelry, such as bracelets and earrings (Figures 144 and 145). Incorporating coins into jewelry may be used to signify monetary wealth.

Figure 144.
Modified coin earrings, Mexico, twentieth century. Donated by U.S. Bureau of Customs.

Figure 145.
Modified coin bracelet, United States, twentieth century. Donated by R. S. Wilson.

THE ALLURE OF MONEY

Wealth is not his that has it, but his that enjoys it.
—Benjamin Franklin, American statesman and inventor[1]

Coin collecting is one of the oldest and most popular hobbies in the world. Collectors value coins, notes, and other objects for their beauty, rarity, and connections to people and places. Building a collection is not only about accumulation; it is a means by which individuals learn about history and draw connections between the past and present.

Collectors often remark that they love to hold old coins in their hands and imagine the generations of people who might have spent, treasured, and saved the same coin. It is the human interactions with money that make monetary objects so appealing to many. For some, coin collecting is a pleasing pastime that requires only modest financial investment, but for serious collectors it can be a life's passion and pursuit.

Examining how an individual approaches building his or her own collection can reveal much about a collector's personal interests and identity. Some collectors develop their collections around particular metals, valuing the material used to make a coin as well as the history behind it. For example, Josiah K. Lilly Jr. was solely interested in gold; he acquired both gold coins and gold bars from around the globe, and his collection reflects the great beauty and diversity of these items from ancient times to the twentieth century. Similarly, Paul A. Straub collected only coins made from gold and silver. He worked tirelessly to acquire gold and silver coins from across Europe, spanning about 800 years of European history.

Coins can also be an accessible way to collect national history, and many collectors use their purchases to capture a nation's political and monetary development. Grand Duke Georgii Mikhailovich, a member of the Russian Romanov dynasty, sought to collect and catalog his own national coinage, from thirteenth century silver ingots to skillfully crafted platinum coins made in the nineteenth century. American collector George B. Glover also had an interest in national and regional history, but his passion was not for his own nation's coinage. Instead, he collected Chinese and East Asian coinage, which he acquired while living and working in China during the nineteenth century.

Although many great coin collections result from a long-term commitment to the hobby, others emerge from moments in time and reflect a unique exchange. President Ulysses S. Grant's stunning collection of Japanese coins was born out of a diplomatic exchange—a gift from the Japanese Emperor Meiji to celebrate their meeting in Japan in 1879.

Coin and note collections are not only constructed by individuals; they are also created by institutions. National mints and central banks often establish collections of monetary objects relating to their work. In the United States, the Mint and Treasury both built their own collections, which include some rarities that cannot legally be purchased by private collectors or that are unique. These assemblages reflect the development of American money and, in the case of the Mint's Collection, include coins from around the world, enabling comparison between American and foreign money.

Thanks to the donation of these and many other individual and institutional collections, the Smithsonian's National Numismatic Collection contains some of the rarest and most valuable numismatic objects in the world. Their greatest value, however, is not in their worth but in their ability to connect people to history and help them see the past in new ways.

The Beginnings of Coin Collecting

Archeological and literary evidence indicates that ancient Roman elites may have collected different types of coins; however, the hobby of coin collecting is usually associated with the Renaissance.[2] European elites and royals, such as King Louis XIV of France, actively sought out ancient coins for their private collections (Figures 146–148). Thus, many people refer to coin collecting as the "hobby of kings."

Figure 146.
Louis XIV medal, France, 1674.
Donated by Frederic A. Delano.

Figure 147.
Sestertius coin, Roman Empire, 54–68 CE.

Figure 148.
One shekel coin, Judea, 66–70 CE.
Donated by The Chase Manhattan Bank.

Coin Collecting in the United States

Coin collecting in the United States gained momentum in the mid-nineteenth century, when collectors began attending auctions to purchase historic coins (Figures 149 and 150). The shift in 1857 from a large copper cent, slightly bigger than today's quarter, to the current cent size helped to popularize the hobby because many people suddenly wanted to hold on to the cents they remembered from childhood before the coins left circulation (Figures 151 and 152).[3]

Figure 149.
One dollar die trial coin, United States, 1794. Donated by Norman and Harvey G. Stack.

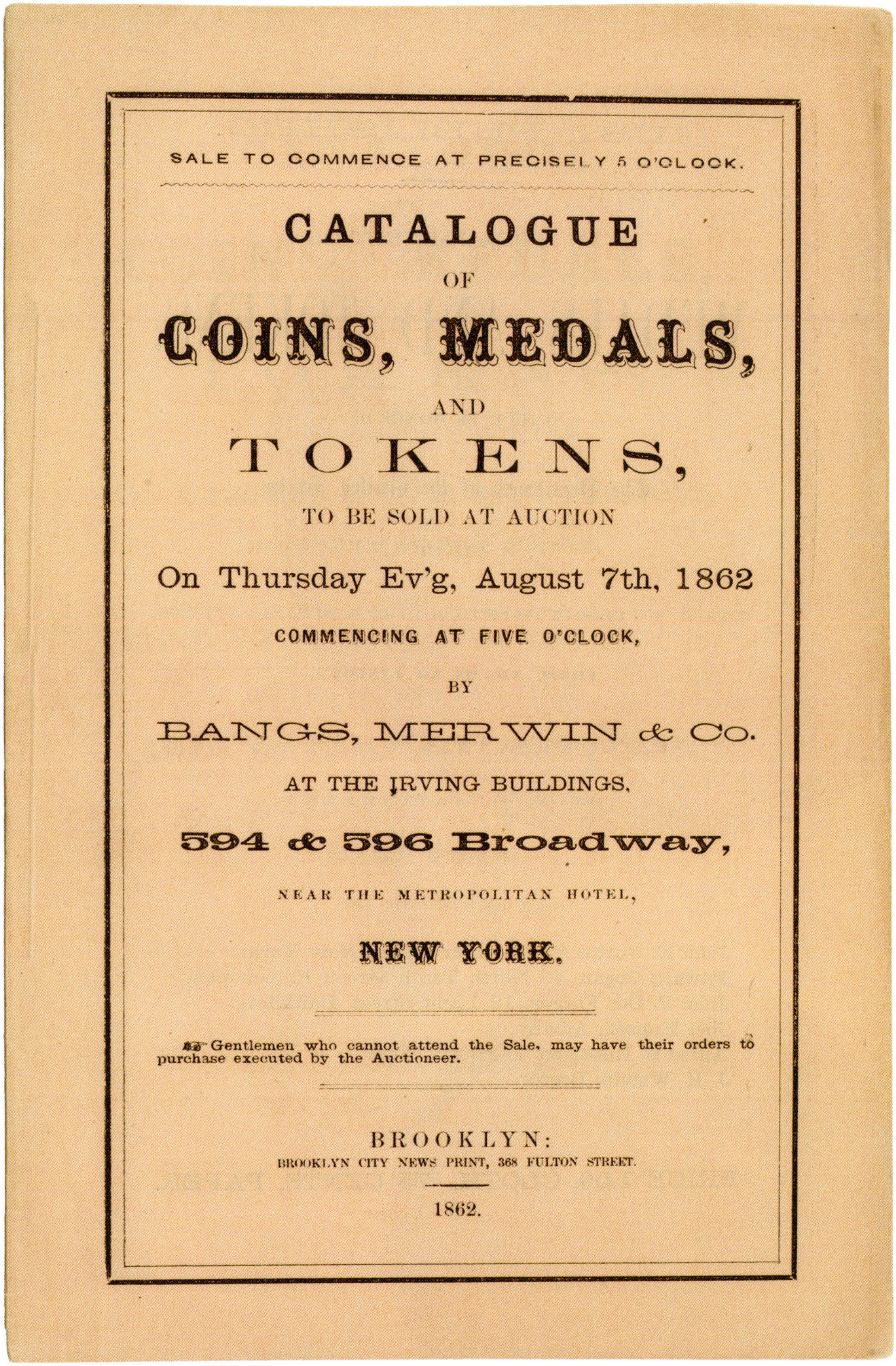

SALE TO COMMENCE AT PRECISELY 5 O'CLOCK.

CATALOGUE

OF

COINS, MEDALS,

AND

TOKENS,

TO BE SOLD AT AUCTION

On Thursday Ev'g, August 7th, 1862

COMMENCING AT FIVE O'CLOCK,

BY

BANGS, MERWIN & Co.

AT THE IRVING BUILDINGS,

594 & 596 Broadway,

NEAR THE METROPOLITAN HOTEL,

NEW YORK.

☞ Gentlemen who cannot attend the Sale, may have their orders to purchase executed by the Auctioneer.

BROOKLYN:
BROOKLYN CITY NEWS PRINT, 368 FULTON STREET.

1862.

Figure 150.
Auction catalog, United States, 1862.
Donated by Kolbe and Fanning Numismatic Booksellers.

Figure 151.
"Large" one cent coin, United States, 1857. Transfer from U.S. Mint.

Figure 152.
One cent coin, United States, 1857. Donated by The Chase Manhattan Bank.

Popularizing Coin Collecting in the United States

The U.S. Mint has played an important role in popularizing the hobby of coin collecting in America. By creating commemorative coins and series, such as the one dollar coins featuring American presidents (Figure 153) and the popular 50 State Quarters, the U.S. Mint has provided an affordable gateway to the hobby for many collectors.

Figure 153.
One dollar coin, United States, 2008. Transfer from U.S. Mint.

Coin Collecting Societies

Coin collectors often meet to discuss their finds and learn from each other. The American Numismatic Society was founded in 1858.[4] The establishment of the American Numismatic Association followed in 1891, and the organization's periodical, *The Numismatist*, helped to promote the hobby (Figure 154). Today the American Numismatic Association has more than 25,000 members.[5]

Figure 154.
The Numismatist, *United States, 1904. Donated by Kolbe and Fanning Numismatic Booksellers.*

Collecting Morgan Dollars

U.S. silver dollars minted between 1878 and 1921 are often called Morgan dollars because they were designed by U.S. Mint engraver George T. Morgan. They are no longer in circulation and have become very popular with coin collectors—so popular, in fact, that they are one of the most collected historic U.S. coins. Collector Jack Lee built one of the finest sets of Morgan dollars ever assembled. The one dollar coin from 1888 shown in Figure 155 is from his private collection, and its holder bears his signature.

Figure 155.
One dollar coin in holder, United States, 1888.

COLLECTING INTERNATIONAL GOLD AND SILVER COINS: THE LILLY AND STRAUB COLLECTIONS

Collecting the World's Gold

Josiah K. Lilly Jr., chairman of the American pharmaceutical company Eli Lilly and Co., was an avid collector of many things, but his interest in coins was focused solely on gold (Figure 156). Between 1951 and his death in 1966, he carefully acquired 6,125 gold coins, one of the finest collections in the world.

Figure 156.
Josiah K. Lilly Jr. Photo courtesy of The Lilly Library, Indiana University, Bloomington, Indiana.

The Josiah K. Lilly Jr. Collection

The Lilly Collection is now part of the National Numismatic Collection. An act of Congress in 1968 brought the coins from Lilly's estate to the Smithsonian. This acquisition contained 1,227 U.S. gold coins, including the very rare five dollar gold coin of 1822 and a unique Brasher half doubloon coin of 1787 (Figures 157 and 158).[6]

Figure 157.
Brasher half doubloon coin, United States, 1787. Donated by Estate of Josiah K. Lilly Jr.

Figure 158.
Five dollar coin, United States, 1822. Donated by Estate of Josiah K. Lilly Jr.

Gold from Around the World

Lilly's interest in gold coins began with seventeenth- and eighteenth-century doubloons from Spanish colonies in Latin America. Over time he developed an interest in gold coins from around the world. His collection includes rare ancient and modern coins from Latin America, East Asia, the Middle East, Africa, and Europe (Figures 159–164).

Figure 159.
Eight escudo coin, Peru, 1708. Donated by Estate of Josiah K. Lilly Jr.

Figure 160.
Two stater coin, Macedon, 336–323 BCE. Donated by Estate of Josiah K. Lilly Jr.

Figure 161.
One hundred ducat coin, Poland, 1621. Donated by Estate of Josiah K. Lilly Jr.

Figure 162.
One and a half ducat coin, Zierikzee (the Netherlands), 1576. Donated by Estate of Josiah K. Lilly Jr.

Figure 163.
Five toman coin, Persia, circa 1896. Donated by Estate of Josiah K. Lilly Jr.

Figure 164.
Twenty won coin, Korea, 1906. Donated by Estate of Josiah K. Lilly Jr.

The Paul A. Straub Collection

Paul A. Straub donated his collection of approximately 5,650 European gold and silver coins from the fourteenth to the twentieth century to the National Numismatic Collection in the 1950s (Figures 165–167).[7] Straub was passionate about developing his collection with the intention of filling gaps in the Smithsonian's holdings. He sought coins that he believed would be so impressive that they would inspire a feeling of pride in the national collection.[8] His donation is regarded as a cornerstone of the National Numismatic Collection's international holdings.

Figure 165.
Five ducat coin, Hamburg (Germany), 1679. Donated by Paul A. Straub.

Figure 166.
Fifty zecchino coin, Venice (Italy), 1779–1789. Donated by Paul A. Straub.

Figure 167.
Ten ducat coin, Czechoslovakia, 1934. Donated by Paul A. Straub.

Straub's Silver

Paul A. Straub collected both gold and silver coins, but he believed that they should be displayed separately. He thought that large silver coins, such as the bulky six thaler coin shown in Figure 168, would overshadow small, delicately engraved gold coins in his collection.[9]

Figure 168.
Six thaler coin, Brunswick (Germany), circa 1679. Donated by Paul A. Straub.

COLLECTING NATIONAL HISTORY: RUSSIA, CHINA, AND THE OTTOMAN EMPIRE

Russian Coinage and Grand Duke Georgii Mikhailovich

The Smithsonian holds the most complete collection of Russian coins and medals outside of Russia. The bulk of this collection was assembled by Grand Duke Georgii Mikhailovich (Figure 169). He had a lifelong commitment to collecting and documenting Russian coinage and published the most comprehensive work ever written on the topic.[10]

Figure 169.
Grand Duke Georgii Mikhailovich.

The Mikhailovich Collection

Grand Duke Georgii Mikhailovich was separated from his collection during the Russian Revolution of 1917.[11] The collection changed hands multiple times in Europe before it ended up on the U.S. coin market and was purchased by Lammot du Pont, whose son donated it to the Smithsonian in the 1950s. The collection includes early Russian metal money, such as the thirteenth century silver ingot, called a grivna, shown in Figure 170.

Figure 170.
Grivna, Russia, thirteenth century.
Donated by Willis H. du Pont.

Russian Coinage of the Romanov Dynasty

Grand Duke Georgii Mikhailovich painstakingly collected the coinage of the House of Romanov, Russia's second imperial dynasty, which ruled from 1613 to 1917. The history of this powerful family can be traced through the images of the emperors and empresses, their families, and their insignia depicted on the coins in Figures 171–176.

Figure 171.
Two ruble coin, Russia, 1726.
Donated by Willis H. du Pont.

Figure 172.
Half poltina coin plate, Russia,
1726. Donated by Willis H. du Pont.

Figure 173.
One ruble coin, Russia, 1740.
Donated by Willis H. du Pont.

Figure 174.
Ten ruble coin, Russia, 1762.
Donated by Willis H. du Pont.

Figure 175.
One and a half ruble coin, Russia, 1835. Donated by Willis H. du Pont.

Figure 176.
Twelve ruble coin, Russia, 1840. Donated by Willis H. du Pont.

The Constantine Ruble

The Constantine ruble is one of the rarest Russian coins (Figure 177). It depicts Russian Grand Duke Constantine Pavlovich, who was expected to ascend to the throne in 1825. He never came to power, having relinquished his succession rights in 1823 because of his controversial marriage, and the coin never circulated.

Figure 177.
One ruble pattern coin, Russia, 1825. Donated by Willis H. du Pont.

The Glover Collection of Chinese Coins

George B. Glover was an official of the Chinese Imperial Maritime Customs Service, an agency in China set up in 1854 to collect taxes on maritime trade.[12] Over the course of his career he amassed a significant collection of East Asian coins. In 1897, he donated 2,025 objects from his collection to the Smithsonian.[13] These coins reflect the breadth and quality of his Chinese coin collection, which spans more than 2,300 years (Figure 178–180).

Figure 178. Knife, China, fifth–third century BCE*. Donated by George B. Glover.*

Figure 179. Spade, China, fourth–third century BCE*. Donated by George B. Glover.*

Figure 180. Ch'ing Dynasty coin, China, 1644–1662. Donated by George B. Glover.

Collecting Ottoman History

The powerful Ottoman Empire lasted from the fifteenth through the early twentieth century, dominating much of southeast Europe and Asia Minor. The National Numismatic Collection holds around 6,000 coins documenting its rich numismatic history. They are gifts from multiple collectors, including Catherine Bullowa, and Raymond and Meryem Hebert, who specialized in different periods (Figures 181 and 182).

Figure 181. Kharub coin, Ottoman Tunis, circa 1852. Donated by Catherine Bullowa.

Figure 182. Qurush coin, Ottoman Constantinople, circa 1731–1732. Donated by Raymond and Meryem Hebert.

COLLECTING AND DIPLOMACY: THE ULYSSES S. GRANT COLLECTION

A Diplomatic Gift from Japan

Ulysses S. Grant traveled the world after his presidency ended in 1877. To mark his visit to Japan in 1879, Grant gifted the Japanese emperor a horse, and in return, the emperor sent him the Japanese coins shown in Figures 183–186.[14] Some may have been made principally for collectors or for ceremonial purposes. The gift exchange reflected the growing relationship between the United States and Japan. Grant's wife, Julia, donated this rare collection to the Smithsonian after his death in 1885.

Figure 183. Commemorative coin, Japan, 1580–1590. Donated by Julia Grant.

Figure 184. Commemorative coin, Japan, 1586–1587. Donated by Julia Grant.

Figure 185. Goryoban coin, Japan, 1837. Donated by Julia Grant.

Figure 186. Oban coin, Japan, 1860. Donated by Julia Grant.

AMERICAN RARITIES: COLLECTIONS OF THE U.S. MINT AND THE U.S. TREASURY

Pattern Coins from the U.S. Mint

The National Numismatic Collection holds historic coins from the U.S. Mint, which transferred approximately 18,300 coins in 1923 and many more since.[15] This large collection includes pattern coins that the U.S. Mint produced to test new designs before approving them for release. The twenty dollar pattern coin from 1849 is the only one of its kind (Figure 187).

Figure 187.
Twenty dollar "Double Eagle" pattern coin, United States, 1849.
Transfer from U.S. Mint.

The 1933 Double Eagle

In 1933, the United States minted 445,500 twenty dollar gold coins, also referred to as double eagles (Figure 188). Before they entered circulation, the government ordered the U.S. Mint to melt them down to conserve national gold stocks. The U.S. Mint chose to preserve two as part of its collection of record and later transferred them to the Smithsonian. Others are thought to have been smuggled from the U.S. Mint. The Secret Service actively seeks information about illicit ownership of these coins; one, however, is legally held in private hands.

Figure 188.
Twenty dollar "Double Eagle" coin, United States, 1933. Transfer from U.S. Mint.

Private Issues Collected by the U.S. Mint

The discovery of gold in California in 1848 provided the raw material for private minters to create their own gold coins, called private issues. The coin in Figure 189 was minted by the Mormons in Utah in 1849. It was subsequently collected by the U.S. Mint and transferred to the National Numismatic Collection, helping to preserve the history of the American gold rush.

Figure 189.
Twenty dollar private issue coin, United States, 1849. Transfer from U.S. Mint.

Proof Coins from the U.S. Mint

The U.S. Mint produces proof coins with special surfaces for collection by museums and coin enthusiasts (Figure 190). These pieces are made with dies that are polished to create mirrorlike fields on coins, distinguishing proofs from regular coins. Proofs are sought after by coin collectors and sold above face value.

Figure 190.
Ten dollar proof coin, United States, 1838. Transfer from U.S. Mint.

The Famous 1804 Silver Dollars

Eight silver dollars bearing the year 1804 were created in the 1830s solely for government use as gifts to foreign dignitaries. They were part of a wider effort to strengthen international commercial relationships. These rare coins were popular among U.S. Mint employees, some of whom secretly produced additional 1804 dollars for personal use or sale to collectors.[16] The National Numismatic Collection is the only collection that holds both the original 1804 dollar, categorized as Class I, and two unofficial versions made by U.S. Mint employees, categorized as Classes II (Figure 191) and III.

Figure 191.
One dollar coin (Class II), United States, circa 1858–1860. Transfer from U.S. Mint.

The Treasury Collection

These notes are thought to be uncollectable because of their rarity. They were donated to the National Numismatic Collection as part of the U.S. Department of the Treasury's collection of reference. The 10,000 dollar note shown in Figure 192 is not thought to be held in private hands, the 100 dollar note in Figure 193 is illegal for a private individual to own because it was issued solely for use in the Federal Reserve system, and the 500 dollar note in Figure 194 with three signatures is the only one of its kind.

Figure 192.
Ten thousand dollar gold certificate, United States, 1928. Donated by U.S. Department of the Treasury.

Figure 193.
One hundred dollar gold certificate, United States, 1934. Donated by U.S. Department of the Treasury.

Figure 194.
Five hundred dollar silver certificate, United States, 1878. Donated by U.S. Department of the Treasury.

NEW RESEARCH TRAJECTORIES AND COLLECTING INITIATIVES

The Value of Money seeks to highlight the National Numismatic Collection's diversity, richness, and unique strengths in the hope of inspiring renewed interest and new research trajectories related to its holdings. The collection is ripe for use by historians, art historians, anthropologists, and archeologists of countless places and periods looking for evocative sources for the study of money and economy and also for studies of politics, culture, society, and technology. The global nature of the collection offers the material needed for regional and comparative studies as well as research on connections between places and periods and the flows of money across geographic and political boundaries.

The potential to conduct research from an international or global perspective in one place is made possible by the individual and institutional collections donated to the Smithsonian over the last century and a half. The presence of so many individual collections makes it an ideal destination for research on the practice of collecting, with material that would aid in the development of a deeper understanding of who collects money with regard to age, gender, and socioeconomic status, how individuals and institutions develop an approach to collecting, and what parts of the story of money remain uncollected or are uncollectible.

Indeed, digital technologies of money present a new challenge and opportunity for both collection and display. The shift from physical to digital transactions will require new and innovative approaches, and the National Numismatic Collection seeks to engage researchers in the development of new ideas. While working to collect the present and the future, both the digital and the physical, the National Numismatic Collection continues to document the past by partnering with individuals and institutions, building on areas of strength, and creating new areas of specialism.

The National Numismatic Collection has much to contribute to the Smithsonian's mission to support the "increase and diffusion of knowledge," mandated by its benefactor, the Englishman James Smithson. Experts in specialist areas of numismatics and researchers from across the humanities and sciences are encouraged to help enliven this powerful collection through individual and collaborative inquiry.

ACKNOWLEDGMENTS

It is said that in creating new works, we stand on the shoulders of giants. I gratefully acknowledge the numismatic scholars and historians as well as my curatorial predecessors and colleagues whose work inspired and contributed to *The Value of Money* exhibition and book. It is a privilege to be able to connect their ideas to the objects in the National Numismatic Collection.

I express my deep appreciation to the whole *The Value of Money* team at the National Museum of American History, with special thanks to Jennifer Jones for her commitment to this project. I am very grateful to Hillery York for her dedication, creative contributions, and perceptive advice at every stage in the curatorial and writing processes. I thank Karen Lee and Robyn Einhorn for helping to lay the groundwork for the exhibition in its early stages and Leslie Poster for her exceptional work editing the exhibition script. I also thank our director, John Gray, and our associate director of curatorial affairs, David Allison, for their guidance and enthusiasm for this project.

The Value of Money benefitted from the help of a superb group of interns, including Samantha Hatton, Aimee Hart, Skyler Rachlin, and Mary Noxon. I am especially thankful to Chelsea Hansen and Melissa Ludke for the research support and assistance they provided in the preparation of this book. I also thank Mike O'Connor and Alexia MacClain for their assistance locating sources inside and outside of the Smithsonian's libraries. I warmly thank Helena Wright for sharing her knowledge of the history of the Smithsonian and offering valuable advice throughout this project.

The content of *The Value of Money* was significantly enhanced by the advice and expertise of many numismatists, curators, and historians from around the world. I am very grateful to my colleagues in the Department of Coins and Medals at the British Museum for their generous support and crucial assistance at multiple stages in the project, with special thanks to Philip Attwood, Barrie Cook, Helen Wang, Vesta Curtis, Robert Bracey, Paramdip Khera, and Amelia Dowler. I also received essential guidance and support from Catherine Eagleton and thank her for her mentorship. Bill Maurer shared his expertise on the technologies of money and payment objects, Jere Bacharach and Atom Damali kindly provided assistance identifying and translating Islamic and Ottoman coins, Robert Goler suggested material from the U.S. Mint for inclusion, Abigail

Seldin offered clever curatorial insight, and Sarah Leavitt provided creative and thoughtful advice throughout the project.

The National Numismatic Collection is fortunate to have the support of a community of numismatists with a deep knowledge of and passion for this collection. I thank Andrew Shiva, Jeff Garrett, Q. David Bowers, Peter Huntoon, Joe Daragan, and Casey Noxon for contributing to this project by sharing their expertise and suggesting the inclusion of well-known and lesser-known objects that will excite numismatists and nonnumismatists alike. I also express my gratitude to the people who donated money, resources, and objects to support this project. Without their assistance, *The Value of Money* would not have been possible.

I thank Ginger Strader and her team at the Smithsonian Institution Scholarly Press for their commitment to this book, Jaclyn Nash for taking the beautiful photographs of the objects that appear herein, and Laura McClure for her crucial assistance with procuring contextual images.

I express my heartfelt gratitude to my husband, Alexander Dewar, for his insightful advice and steadfast encouragement throughout this project. I am eternally grateful to my family—Susan Feingold, Russell Feingold, Christine Ferdinand, Jessica Feingold Lieberson, and Jeffery Lieberson—for their guidance and unwavering support. I offer special thanks to my stepfather, Chester Dussault, for reading every word of this book and offering me feedback at a moment's notice. I also honor the memory of three loving mothers—Pearl K. Levine, Sylvia B. Feingold, and Lori L. Stone—who cultivated a passion for learning in their homes that has enriched my life and the lives of so many others.

Finally, my deepest gratitude is to the National Museum of American History and Smithsonian Institution for giving me the opportunity to work with and share this magnificent collection.

NOTES

INTRODUCTION

1. Philip Grierson, *Numismatics* (London: Oxford University Press, 1975), 1.
2. For more detailed information on the objects that comprised the numismatic collection during the nineteenth century, see Vladimir Clain-Stefanelli, *History of the National Numismatic Collections* (Washington, D.C.: Smithsonian Institution, 1968), 3–9.
3. Carl Allenbaugh, "The Creation of the Smithsonian: A Stranger's Gift to a New Land Has Paid Great Dividends to Coin Collectors Everywhere," *Coinage,* August 1972, 20.
4. Allenbaugh, "Creation of the Smithsonian," 20.
5. Clain-Stefanelli, *History of the National Numismatic Collections*, 19.
6. For more information on the objects included in the Mint Collection, see Clain-Stefanelli, *History of the National Numismatic Collections*, 89–99; Elvira Clain-Stefanelli, "Donors and Donations: The Smithsonian's National Numismatic Collection," in *Perspectives in Numismatics*, ed. Saul B. Needleman (Chicago: Ares, 1986), 254–255.
7. Clain-Stefanelli, *History of the National Numismatic Collections*, 14.
8. The acquisition of the Straub Collection is documented in Clain-Stefanelli, *History of the National Numismatic Collections*, 99–103.
9. Clain-Stefanelli, "Donors and Donations," 255.
10. For a detailed description of the Hall of Monetary History and Medallic Art installed in 1964, see Vladimir Clain-Stefanelli, "Monetary History and Medallic Art at the Smithsonian Institution, Washington, D.C.," *Nvmisma* 75 (July–August 1965): 41–46.
11. Allenbaugh, "Creation of the Smithsonian," 20.
12. Clain-Stefanelli, "Donors and Donations," 257.
13. Elvira Clain-Stefanelli recalls the details of the collections she and Vladimir Clain-Stefanelli acquired in "Donors and Donations," 257–268.
14. For example, see Jeff Garrett, "Brief History of the Smithsonian's National Numismatic Collection," *Coinweek*, 24 May 2013, http://www.coinweek.com/featured-news/brief-history-of-the-smithsonians-national-numismatic-collection/.
15. Elvira Clain-Stefanelli chronicled highlights from The Chase Manhattan Bank Collection in *Highlights from the Money Collection of the Chase Manhattan Bank* (Washington, D.C.: National Museum of History and Technology, 1979).
16. I am grateful to Richard Doty and Nancy Bercaw for their research on the origins of the "Richmond Hoard" and the process through which it came to the Smithsonian.

THE ORIGINS OF MONEY

1. Adam Smith, *Paper Money* (New York: Summit Books, 1981), 61.
2. Joe Cribb, ed., *Money: From Cowrie Shells to Credit Cards* (London: British Museum Publications, 1986), 9.

3. Catherine Eagleton and Jonathan Williams, eds., *Money: A History* (London: British Museum Press, 2007), 218–224.
4. W. H. Furness, *The Island of Stone Money: Uap of the Carolines* (Philadelphia: J. B. Lippincott, 1910), 96.
5. Eagleton and Williams, *Money: A History*, 214.
6. For a detailed description of the text and imagery on the Great Ming Circulating Treasure Note and its historical context, see Neil MacGregor, *A History of the World in 100 Objects* (London: Penguin Books, 2010), 465–469.
7. On the origins and uses of gold weights in West Africa, see Timothy F. Garrard, *Akan Weights and the Gold Trade* (New York: Longman, 1980).
8. On minting coins, see Cribb, *Money*, 88–111.
9. On printing paper money, see Cribb, *Money*, 116–17.

THE INNOVATIONS OF MONEY

1. John Maynard Keynes, *The General Theory of Employment Interest and Money* (New York: Harcourt, Brace, 1936), 293.
2. For cutting-edge research on mobile money and how it is impacting people around the world, consult the white papers published on the website of the Institute for Money, Technology and Financial Inclusion at the University of California, Irvine (http://www.imtfi.uci.edu/), available as of 1 February 2015.

THE MESSAGES OF MONEY

1. This interpretation of the note's imagery is a matter of debate. It can be found in Richard Doty, *America's Money, America's Story*, 2nd ed. (Atlanta: Whitman, 2008), 45.
2. On the use of foreign currencies in colonial America, see Doty, *America's Money, America's Story*, 34–35.
3. Neil MacGregor, *A History of the World in 100 Objects* (London: Penguin Books, 2010), 517.
4. For more on the origins of the word *money*, see Cribb, *Money*, 11.
5. Zvi Stahl, *Jewish Ghettos' and Concentration Camps' Money (1933–1945)* (London: D. Richman Books, 1990), 30; Lance K. Campbell, *Prisoner of War and Concentration Camp Money of the Twentieth Century*, 2nd ed. (Port Clinton, OH: BNR Press, 1993), 102.
6. Stahl, *Jewish Ghettos' and Concentration Camps' Money*, 36 (Łódź), 48–50 (Theresienstadt).
7. For a more detailed description of the imagery on the tortoise hard-times token, see Russell Rulau, *Hard Times Tokens 1832–1844* (Iola, WI: Krause, 2001), 23.

THE ARTISTRY OF MONEY

1. Will Durant, *The Story of Philosophy: The Lives and Opinions of the Greater Philosophers* (New York: Simon and Schuster, 1926), 84.
2. Gene Hessler, *U.S. Essay, Proof and Specimen Notes* (Portage, OH: BNR Press, 1979), 98. On the design of the 1896 silver certificate series, see pages 98–119 of this Hessler work.
3. Mark Van Winkle, "The Sculptor, the President and the Making of a Classic American Coinage," in *The Coinage of Augustus Saint-Gaudens as Illustrated by the Phillip H. Morse Collection*, J. L. Halperin, M. Van Winkle, J. Amato, and G. J. Rohan (Dallas: Ivy Press, 2006), 7. Roosevelt was particularly fond of the high relief of the coins of Alexander the Great. The selection of the objects for Figures 109 and 110 was inspired by those depicted in Van Winkle, "The Sculptor, the President," 8–9.

4. Saint-Gaudens passed away in 1907 and did not complete his design for the U.S. cent coin. The commission was subsequently given to Victor D. Brenner, who designed the famous Lincoln cent (see Figure 87).
5. On production challenges, see Van Winkle, "The Sculptor, the President," 10–11.

THE ALLURE OF MONEY

1. Benjamin Franklin, *Poor Richard's Almanack* (Waterloo, IA: U.S.C. Publishing Co., 1914), 57.
2. On the history of coin collecting during the Renaissance and the eighteenth century, see Elvira E. Clain-Stefanelli, *Numismatics—An Ancient Science: A Survey of Its History* (Washington, D.C.: Smithsonian Institution, 1965), 15–25.
3. Q. David Bowers, "Big Changes in Coin Hobby in 1857 with Introduction of New Cent Design and Founding of Coin Clubs," *Coin World*, 29 July 2014, http://www.coinworld.com/insights/Big-changes-in-coin-hobby-in-1857-and-1858.html#.
4. More information on the history and activities of the American Numismatic Society is available on their website (http://www.numismatics.org, accessed 1 February 2015).
5. More information on the history and activities of the American Numismatic Association is available on their website (http://www.money.org, accessed 1 February 2015).
6. Clain-Stefanelli, "Donors and Donations," 265.
7. Clain-Stefanelli, *History of the National Numismatic Collections*, 14.
8. Clain-Stefanelli, "Donors and Donations," 255.
9. Paul A. Straub wrote a letter on 12 January 1942 stating his display preferences for gold and silver coins. An excerpt of this letter is reproduced in Clain-Stefanelli, *History of the National Numismatic Collections*, 101.
10. Natalya Smirnova, "Grand Duke Georgii Mikhailovich (1863–1919)," *Compte Rendu.* 58 (2011), 27 (http://inc-cin.org/assets/pdf/compterendu/compte-rendu-58-2011.pdf, accessed 21 April 2015). The National Numismatic Collection holds a copy of Mikhailovich's *Corpus of Russian Coins.*
11. There are varying accounts of the whereabouts of Mikhailovich's collection during and immediately following the Russian Revolution of 1917. For one account of these events, see Smirnova, "Grand Duke Georgii Mikhailovich," 30–31.
12. J. H. S. Lockhart, *The Currency from the Farther East: From the Earliest Times to the Present Day* (Hong Kong: Noronha, 1895), 1:vii.
13. Clain-Stefanelli, *History of the National Numismatic Collections*, 9.
14. Clain-Stefanelli, *History of the National Numismatic Collections*, 88.
15. Clain-Stefanelli, "Donors and Donations," 254.
16. The 1804 silver dollar is a controversial coin because of disagreement over the details of its background and legal status. The debate is covered in Eric P. Newman and Kenneth E. Bressett, *The Fantastic 1804 Dollar: A Commemorative Reissue of the Famous Story of the "King of Coins"* (Atlanta: Whitman, 2009).

BIBLIOGRAPHY BY TOPIC

THE ORIGINS OF MONEY

The History of Money and Field of Numismatics

Burnett, Andrew. *Coins.* Berkley: University of California Press, 1991.

Cribb, Joe, ed. *Money: From Cowrie Shells to Credit Cards.* London: British Museum Publications, 1986.

Eagleton, Catherine, and Jonathan Williams, eds. *Money: A History.* London: British Museum Press, 2007.

Galbraith, John K. *Money: Whence It Came, Whence It Went.* Boston: Houghton Mifflin, 1975.

Grierson, Philip. *Numismatics.* London: Oxford University Press, 1975.

Porteous, John. *Coins in History.* New York: Putnam, 1969.

Vilar, Pierre. *A History of Gold and Money, 1450 to 1920.* Brooklyn: Verso, 1984.

Shell Money

Hogendorn, Jan, and Marion Johnson. *The Shell Money of the Slave Trade.* Cambridge: Cambridge University Press, 1986.

Shell, Marc. *Wampum and the Origins of American Money.* Urbana: University of Illinois Press, 2013.

Stone Money from the Island of Yap

Furness, W. H. *The Island of Stone Money: Uap of the Carolines.* Philadelphia: J. B. Lippincott, 1910.

———. "The Stone Money of Uap, West Caroline Islands." *Transactions of the Department of Archaelogym University of Pennsylvania Museum* 1 (1904): 51–60.

Gillilland, Cora Lee C. *The Stone Money of Yap: A Numismatic Survey.* Washington, D.C.: Smithsonian Institution Press, 1975.

Goldberg, Dror. "Famous Myths of 'Fiat Money.'" *Journal of Money, Credit and Banking* 37, no. 5 (2005): 957–967.

THE INNOVATIONS OF MONEY

Charge and Credit Cards

Hyman, Louis. *Debtor Nation: A History of America in Red Ink.* Princeton, NJ: Princeton University Press, 2011.

Stearns, David L. *Electronic Value Exchange: Origins of the Visa Electronic Payment System.* London: Springer, 2011.

Swartz, Lana. "Gendered Transactions: Identity and Payment at Midcentury." *Women's Studies Quarterly* 42, nos. 1–2 (2014): 137–153.

Modern Payment Artifacts

Maurer, Bill, and Lana Swartz, eds. *Payment Objects: Explorations with Transactional Things*. Cambridge: MIT Press, forthcoming.

Mobile Money

Donovan, Kevin. "Mobile Money for Financial Inclusion." In *Information and Communications for Development*, ed. T. Kelly and M. Minges, pp. 61–73. Washington, D.C.: World Bank, 2012.

Kendall, Jake, Bill Maurer, Phillip Machoka, and Clara Veniard. "An Emerging Platform: From Money Transfer System to Mobile Money Ecosystem." *Innovations: Technology, Governance, Globalization* 6, no. 4 (2012): 49–64

Maurer, Bill. "Mobile Money: Communication, Consumption and Change in the Payments Space." *Journal of Development Studies* 48, no. 5 (2012): 589–604.

Polymer Banknotes

Eu, Peter, Ben Chiew, and Julian Chee. *World Polymer Banknotes*. Malaysia: Eureka Metro Sdn. Bhd., 2005.

National Currencies

Helleiner, Eric. "National Currencies and National Identities." *American Behavioral Scientist* August 41, no. 10 (1998): 1409–1436.

The Euro

Marsh, David. *The Euro: The Battle for the New Global Currency*. Rev ed. New Haven, CT: Yale University Press, 2011.

THE MESSAGES OF MONEY

Early American Coins

Doty, Richard. *America's Money, America's Story*. 2nd ed. Atlanta: Whitman, 2008.

Mossman, Philip L. *Money of the American Colonies and Confederation: A Numismatic, Economic, and Historical Correlation*. New York: The American Numismatic Society, 1993.

American Paper Money

Criswell, Grover C. *Comprehensive Catalog of Confederate Paper Money*. Port Clinton, OH: BNR Press, 1996.

Doty, Richard. *Pictures from a Distant Country: Seeing America through Old Paper Money*. Atlanta: Whitman, 2013.

Friedberg, Arthur L., and Ira S. Friedberg. *Paper Money of the United States: A Complete Illustrated Guide with Valuations*. 20th ed. Clifton, NJ: Coin and Currency Institute, 2013.

Newman, Eric P. *Early Paper Money of America*. 5th ed. Iola, WI: Krause, 2008.

Counterfeiting in the United States

Mihm, Stephen. *A Nation of Counterfeiters: Capitalists, Con Men, and the Making of the United States*. Cambridge, MA: Harvard University Press, 2007.

Mossman, Philip L. *From Crime to Punishment: Counterfeit and Debased Currencies in Colonial and Pre-Federal America*. New York: American Numismatic Society, 2013.

Scott, Kenneth. *Counterfeiting in Colonia America*. Philadelphia: University of Pennsylvania Press, 2000.

Concentration Camp and Military Currencies from the Second World War

Campbell, Lance K. *Prisoner of War and Concentration Camp Money of the Twentieth Century*. 2nd ed. Port Clinton, OH: BNR Press, 1993.

Schwan, C. Frederick, and Joseph E. Boling. *World War II Remembered*. Port Clinton, OH: BNR Press, 1995.

Stahl, Zvi. *Jewish Ghettos' and Concentration Camps' Money (1933–1945)*. London: D. Richman Books, 1990.

THE ARTISTRY OF MONEY

Greek Coins

Carradice, Ian. *Greek Coins*. Austin: University of Texas, 1995.

Carradice, Ian, and Martin Price. *Coinage of the Greek World*. London: Seaby, 1988.

Jenkins, Kenneth. *Coins of Greek Sicily*. 2nd ed. London: British Museum Press, 1976.

Metcalf, William E. *The Oxford Handbook of Greek and Roman Coinage*. New York: Oxford University Press, 2012.

The Life and Work of Augustus Saint-Gaudens

Dryfhort, John H. *The Work of Augustus Saint-Gaudens*. Hanover, NH: University Press of New England, 1982.

Hall Tharp, Louise. *Saint-Gaudens and the Gilded Era*. Boston: Little, Brown, 1969.

Halperin, James, Mark Van Winkle, Jon Amato, and Gregory J. Rohan. *The Coinage of Augustus Saint-Gaudens as Illustrated by the Phillip H. Morse Collection*. Dallas: Ivy Press, 2006.

Moran, Michael F. *Striking Change: The Great Artistic Collaboration of Theodore Roosevelt and Augustus Saint-Gaudens*. Atlanta: Whitman, 2008.

Paper Money Design

Hessler, Gene. *U.S. Essay, Proof and Specimen Notes*. Portage, OH: BNR Press, 1979.

Standish, David. *The Art of Money: The History and Design of Paper Currency from Around the World*. San Francisco: Chronicle Books, 2000.

THE ALLURE OF MONEY

Coin Collecting and Popular American Coins

Bowers, Q. David. *American Numismatics before the Civil War, 1760–1860*. Wolfeboro, NH: Bowers and Merena Galleries, 1998.

———. "Big Changes in Coin Hobby in 1857 with Introduction of New Cent Design and Founding of Coin Clubs." *Coin World*, 29 July 2014. http://www.coinword.com/insights/Big-changes-in-coin-hobby-in-1857-and-1858.html#.

Clain-Stefanelli, Elvira E. *Numismatics—An Ancient Science: A Survey of Its History*. Washington, D.C.: Smithsonian Institution, 1965.

Garrett, Jeff. *100 Greatest U.S. Coins*. 4th ed. Atlanta: Whitman, 2014.

Guth, Ron, and Jeff Garrett. *United States Coinage: A Study by Type*. Atlanta: Whitman: 2005.

Yeoman, R. S. *A Guide Book of United States Coins 2015*. 68th ed. Atlanta: Whitman, 2014.

The Josiah K. Lilly Jr. Collection

Bardes, Herbert C. "Lilly Gold Offer Moves Forward." *New York Times*, 24 September 1967.

Clain-Stefanelli, Elvira. "Donors and Donations: The Smithsonian's National Numismatic Collection." In *Perspectives in Numismatics*, ed. Saul B. Needleman, pp. 251–268. Chicago: Ares, 1986.

Gillilland, Cory. *Sylloge of the United States Holdings in the National Numismatic Collection of the Smithsonian Institution: Gold Coins, 1785–1834*. Smithsonian Institution Press: Washington, D.C., 1992.

Stevens, Larry. "D-Day for the Lilly Gold." *Coinage* 5, no. 6 (1969): 52–57.

The Georgii Mikhailovich Collection

Smirnova, Natalya. "Grand Duke Georgii Mikhailovich (1863–1919)." *Compte Rendu* 58 (2011): 27–31.

The George B. Glover Collection

Lockhart, J. H. S. *The Currency from the Farther East: From the Earliest Times to the Present Day*. Volumes 1–2. Hong Kong: Noronha, 1895.

The Ulysses S. Grant Collection

Clain-Stefanelli, Vladimir. *History of the National Numismatic Collections*. Washington, D.C.: Smithsonian Institution, 1968.

The Paul A. Straub Collection

Clain-Stefanelli, Vladimir. *History of the National Numismatic Collections*. Washington, D.C.: Smithsonian Institution, 1968.

The History of the U.S. Mint and Its Collection

Clain-Stefanelli, Vladimir. *History of the National Numismatic Collections*. Washington, D.C.: Smithsonian Institution, 1968.

Orosz, Joel, and Leonard Augsburger. *The Secret History of the First U.S. Mint*. Atlanta: Whitman, 2011.

Taxy, Donald. *The U.S. Mint and Coinage: An Illustrated History From 1776 to the Present*. New York: Arco, 1966.

The 1933 Double Eagle

Tripp, David. *Illegal Tender: Gold, Greed, and the Mystery of the Lost 1933 Double Eagle*. New York: Free Press, 2004.

The 1804 Silver Dollars

Newman, Eric P., and Kenneth E. Bressett. *The Fantastic 1804 Dollar: A Commemorative Reissue of the Famous Story of the "King of Coins."* Atlanta: Whitman, 2009.

ADDITIONAL REFERENCES

Allenbaugh, Carl. "The Creation of the Smithsonian: A Stranger's Gift to a New Land Has Paid Great Dividends to Coin Collectors Everywhere." *Coinage,* August 1972: 15–20, 92–93.

Clain-Stefanelli, Elvira. *Highlights from the Money Collection of the Chase Manhattan Bank.* Washington, D.C.: National Museum of History and Technology, 1979.

Clain-Stefanelli, Vladimir. "Monetary History and Medallic Art at the Smithsonian Institution, Washington, D.C." *Nvmisma* 75 (July–August 1965): 31–48.

Durant, Will. *The Story of Philosophy: The Lives and Opinions of the Greater Philosophers.* New York: Simon and Schuster, 1926.

Franklin, Benjamin. *Poor Richard's Almanack.* Waterloo, IA: U.S.C. Publishing Co., 1914.

Garrard, Timothy F. *Akan Weights and the Gold Trade.* New York: Longman, 1980.

Garrett, Jeff. "Brief History of the Smithsonian's National Numismatic Collection." *Coinweek*, 24 May 2013. http://www.coinweek.com/featured-news/brief-history-of-the-smithsonians-national-numismatic-collection/.

Keynes, John Maynard. *The General Theory of Employment Interest and Money.* New York: Harcourt, Brace, 1936.

MacGregor, Neil. *A History of the World in 100 Objects.* London: Penguin Books, 2010.

Rulau, Russell. *Hard Times Tokens 1832–1844.* Iola, WI: Krause, 2001.

Smith, Adam. *Paper Money.* New York: Summit Books, 1981.

Van Winkle, Mark. "The Sculptor, the President and the Making of a Classic American Coinage." In *The Coinage of Augustus Saint-Gaudens as Illustrated by the Phillip H. Morse Collection*, J. L. Halperin, M. Van Winkle, J. Amato, and G. J. Rohan, pp. 7–12. Dallas: Ivy Press, 2006.

INDEX

Note: Page numbers referring to images appear in bold.